THE CHEECHAKOES

THE CHEECHAKOES

WAYNE SHORT

drawings by PETER PARNALL

Random House : New York

Few frontiers would have been settled without that special breed of women who have always followed the footsteps of their wandering husbands. This book is for my wife, Barbara, and for Ma, bless her.

ACKNOWLEDGMENT

I doubt if anyone but a complete egotist would ever attempt to write an autobiographical book without encouragement from another. I certainly would not have attempted this one if it had not been for Rogers Terrill, who did not live to see it completed.

W. S.

CONTENTS

1   ALASKA!   3

2   THE NEW LAND   12

3   GREENHORN FISHERMEN   32

4   PAP BUYS A BOAT   51

5   THE BROWN BEAR   64

6   BEAR, AND MORE BEAR   77

7   WINTER   91

8   A TRIP TO TOWN   107

9   THE SEAL HUNTERS   123

10   SPRING AGAIN   145

11   OVERBOARD!   154

12   THE SILVER HORDE   167

13   DUKE QUITS SCHOOL   179

14   MAILBOAT   187

15   THE TRAPPERS   195

16   WE MOVE TO BARANOF   218

17   A BRIDE COMES NORTH   236

THE CHEECHAKOES

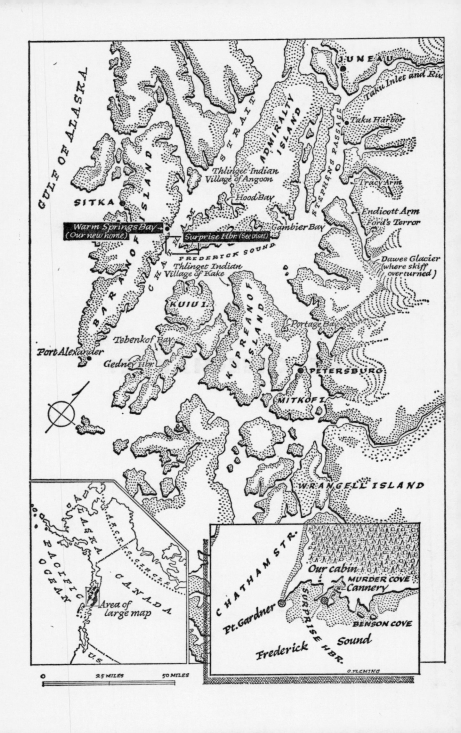

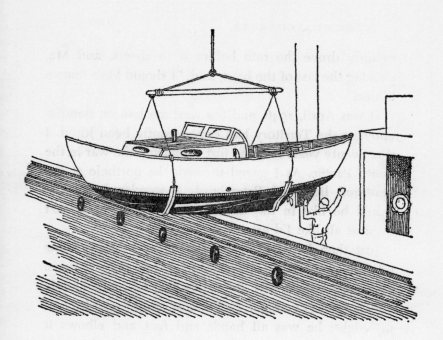

1
ALASKA!

It was near midnight when the *North Sea* eased through the last stretch of treacherous Wrangell Narrows, and came slowly in toward the Alaska Steamship Company dock in Petersburg, Alaska. A gusty south-

(3)

easterly drove the rain before it in sheets, and Ma, packing the last of the bags, said, "I should have known better!"

It was April, 1946, and the wartime ban on families entering the Territory had only recently been lifted. I was twenty years old, and just back from the war in the South Pacific. As I gazed through the porthole at the scattered lights of Petersburg, I wondered what it would be like in the daylight. So far, Alaska hadn't been at all like I'd expected.

Just then Pap and my two younger brothers came into the stateroom, rain dripping from their slickers. Duke, at sixteen, was almost six feet tall, and Dutch, only two years younger, had almost caught up with him in height; he was all hands and feet and elbows it seemed, but there was in him the promise of a big man when he filled out.

Pap, small and wiry, and tough as whang leather, shook the rain from his dress Stetson, then moved to the open port to look back into the night from which we'd come. He stood there silent with his thoughts, and as I watched the play of expression cross his weathered features, I knew what he was thinking. Behind him lay the hard, bitter years of the depression, the frustration of trying to fit into a modern society which he detested, the lifelong search that had touched so many, many places, yet none of them had been the one that he had been looking for.

Pap turned away from the porthole then, and the strange look was gone from his face. "They're getting the lines onto the dock," he said. "Wayne, you take Duke with you and stand by the *Resolute.* I talked to the mate, and as soon as the passengers have disembarked they'll lift the *Resolute* off deck and set her into the water. You and Duke go aboard and be ready. When you are in the water, start the engine and throw off the slings, then run her over to the boat harbor."

"Okay," I said, "but where is this boat harbor?"

Pap opened the door and we stepped out to the railing. To our right, and at the foot of the town, there seemed to be several rows of log floats where the small fishing vessels were moored. The dim lights from uptown silhouetted their masts and booms and trolling poles. "There it is," Pap said, pointing. "Find a place to tie the *Resolute* for the night, then come on up to the hotel."

"Which one?"

"There's only one—the Mitkof Hotel."

"All right, Pap."

We stepped back into the stateroom and Pap turned to Ma and said, "Now, then, as soon as the gangplank goes onto the dock we'll carry our bags uptown and get rooms lined up. Then Dutch and I will come back down to the dock and see that all of our things are unloaded."

There came the creaking of blocks on the foredeck, and after a moment Dutch came back inside with Spot, our three-legged terrier, and told us the gangplank was in place and that passengers were going ashore.

"Let's go then," Pap said.

We carried our bags out into the rain and down the side of the ship to the gangplank. Duke and I left the others there, and made our way down the ladder to the foredeck.

The *Resolute* sat on deck in a wooden cradle that was tightly lashed down with cables to keep it from shifting. She was a surplus twenty-two-foot steel-hulled lifeboat we had bought a month before in Port-land, Oregon. We had decked it over and added a plywood cabin. It was powered with a small twenty-five-horsepower Universal gasoline engine. This little vessel would play a big part in getting us settled in Surprise Harbor, an isolated bay on the southern tip of Admiralty Island, some seventy miles by sea from Petersburg. As Duke and I stood by waiting, the mate walked over to ask if we were ready, and I told him we were. He called for a couple of riggers, and they began loosening the cables that held the *Resolute* down.

When the lashings were off, Duke and I climbed aboard and waited as the riggers passed straps beneath the hull and handed them up to us. We shackled them to the cable the winch man lowered from overhead, and at the mate's signal the *Resolute* rose slowly out of its cradle and began to swing over the side. As we were being lowered to the water I went inside the cabin and started the engine.

When I felt the hull settle into the sea I came on deck and looked to see if the engine's water pump had picked up its prime. It had, and I called to Duke on the bow and told him to let his strap go. I unshackled the stern strap. We were ready now. I went inside to the controls and we eased slowly around the towering stern of the *North Sea*. Ahead were the lights of the boat harbor. We moved slowly toward it, trying to make out its indistinct shape in the driving rain.

"I think I see an empty spot," Duke at last called from the bow.

I saw it then too, and eased the *Resolute* toward a place at the float between two fishing boats. We made our lines fast, shut down the engine, then began to walk up the dim float toward the ramp that connected the floats to the dock approach. The night was still black, and the wind and rain lashed at us as we stepped off the approach into the muddy street that led to the main thoroughfare. We turned onto the planked sidewalk and went down the single empty street until we came to the Mitkof Hotel.

That night as I lay in bed I began thinking of all the years we had been working toward this goal.

Coming to Alaska had not been just a capricious move on Pap's part. Our first abortive attempt to migrate to this "Last Frontier" went back fully ten years, when we were then living in Colorado, and Pap heard the government was sending families to settle in the Matanuska Valley near Anchorage. He made out an application, but the quota had already been filled when his name came up.

Typically, Pap said: "I've never liked charity, anyway. We'll pay our own way to Alaska and settle where we please!" But this had been in the middle of the depression, and it was just an idle dream, for our savings were exactly one thin dime that Pap carried in his trousers pocket to keep from being "broke." He was engaged in cutting cedar posts on Grande Mesa and selling them for one cent apiece. I was just ten at the time, but I well remember the hard work it was to load them into a wagon and haul them by team into Delta. We seldom received cash; for the most part we traded for whatever the buyer might have: a few chickens here, a sack of spuds there, a pig, or perhaps a quarter of beef.

But the privations imposed upon him did not make him bitter; rather, they inspired him to seek a place where he could live pretty much off of the land.

In 1936, when he received the second half of his veterans' bonus from World War One, he decided to take the big step. He sold our farm for what he could get, paid his debts, then shipped our belongings to Seattle to await us. We set out for Alaska one fine spring morning in a beat-up Chevrolet sedan, but luck was not with us.

In Eugene, Oregon, Duke, then six years old, began complaining of a pain in his right leg. An examination and subsequent X-ray showed he had osteomyelitis, a bone disease brought on by a previous accident. The ball of his hip joint was almost eaten away by decay. Moving to some isolated spot in Alaska away from medical care was out of the question, so Pap bought a small place up the McKenzie River Valley, and he and Ma began a fight with the doctors to keep them from amputating Duke's leg. Finally they found a doctor who thought the leg might be saved, and Duke began a two-year ordeal in a body cast that reached from his armpits to the ankle of the diseased leg. When at last the cast was taken off, he had to spend the next three years on crutches. The leg had been saved, but we were so hopelessly in debt that Alaska was a long-buried dream.

Then came the war. At least a man could find work. Our finances were beginning to improve by the time I joined the Navy and was sent to the South Pacific.

During the summers of 1944-45, Pap had gone north in salmon season, to work as carpenter for Sebastian and Stuart, a firm that canned and processed salmon at Tyee, in southeastern Alaska. There was something about this country that he had liked. Tyee, in Murder Cove, was on the southern tip of Admiralty Island—about a hundred miles south of Juneau. This was a wilderness like Oregon and Washington had been a century before, isolated country, but it had immense appeal for him.

The most important thing was the fact that a man could live off the land. Deer were plentiful, and would be the mainstay; there was a world of grouse and ptarmigan, ducks, geese. And the sea would give us almost everything else we needed: there were clams and crabs for the taking, salmon and halibut. Pap had watched the commercial trolling boats come in and unload at the cold storage in Murder Cove, and he had been impressed with the money they made from fishing. It was true we didn't know the first thing about commercial fishing, but we could learn. With that in mind we had bought the little steel lifeboat. Pap would work another summer at the cannery, and we boys would try our hand at commercial fishing.

In the meantime we had a lot of work ahead of us. Pap had looked the country over the previous summer, and at last decided the ideal building site was in Surprise Harbor, just around the peninsula from the Tyee cannery in Murder Cove. We would build our house, stake off enough ground for a garden and outbuildings, and the Forest Service would then come and survey the homesite. It would cost us five dollars a year for the homesite permit, and at the end of a certain length of time we would be eligible to apply for patent on this land.

Pap had made arrangements with a local fisherman to meet us in Petersburg and show us the way out to Surprise Harbor. In the morning we would go down to the harbor and look for his boat, the *Chester L.*

Now, as I lay in bed with these thoughts in mind, I found it hard to believe that after all these years we were at last realizing the dream which had lain dormant so long. Looking back, however, I know that Ma must have been broken-hearted to leave our home in Oregon and set off to the Alaskan wilderness, on what she called "one of Walter's wild-goose chases." But she could not hope to hold out long against the desires of Pap and us three boys.

I got so excited just thinking about it all, that I turned on the light and got up. Duke, sleeping in the bed across from me, awoke and asked, "What's up?"

I took the nautical chart from my suitcase and spread it out on the floor for the hundredth time. "I just wanted to look at it again," I said. Together we retraced our route by sea to Surprise Harbor, stopping to study the bays and inlets on the way, and to check the contour and elevation of the mountains.

Finally, Duke got sleepy and went back to bed. I carefully rolled the chart and put it back into my suitcase. I climbed back in bed and turned the light out, and tried to force myself to sleep. One thing I was certain of: ahead of us lay a great new land.

2
THE NEW LAND

The next morning we were up by seven. We dressed and descended to the street. Petersburg was a little frontier fishing town, and its population of somewhat more than a thousand ran pretty much to Norwegians.

A single dirt street ran through the business district and, according to a resident, was either ankle-deep mud or dust, depending on the weather. Besides the hotel, there was a restaurant, movie house, post office, several groceries, a bank, three bars, and a service station and machine shop; on the waterfront was a large cold-storage plant and a salmon cannery, as well as a shrimp and crab cannery. A man in the hotel lobby had told me that the road extended only a few miles on the Narrows side of the town.

It was still raining and we obliquely crossed the muddy thoroughfare to the restaurant for breakfast, where we had the best coffee I had ever tasted. I noticed that whenever a customer stepped inside and seated himself he was first served a steaming cup of coffee without a word and *then* asked what else he'd like.

After a big breakfast of ham and eggs we stepped outside into the rain once again. The wind seemed to have abated, but the rain was relentless. As we walked down the boardwalk we met a strange-looking man standing in front of the shrimp and crab cannery: he looked exactly like the pictures you see of the old-time Klondike men of fifty years ago. He was dressed in boot pants and leather puttees, and he wore one of those wide-brimmed miner's hats. He had a handle-bar moustache and goatee, and across his vest was a string of gold nuggets on a watch chain. His eyes twinkled as

he surveyed us, and he gallantly lifted the immense hat
and bowed to Ma.

Earl Ohmer, he said his name was, and he shook
hands all around as Pap introduced us. We talked for
half an hour of the country, and as we parted Ohmer's
last words were: "You boys watch out for those Admiralty Island brown bear!"

We had talked the cook at the restaurant out of a
sack of scraps for Spot, and now Ma said she would go
back to the hotel and feed him. The rest of us turned
toward the boat harbor to check the *Resolute* and see if
the *Chester L* had arrived.

After pumping the *Resolute,* we made a round of
the boat floats, and presently Pap said, "There's the
Chester L." She was perhaps forty-two feet in length,
and was rigged as a troller. Smoke spiralled from the
foc'sle chimney, and the odor of frying bacon came
through the open wheelhouse door.

We stepped aboard and Pap stuck his head into the
doorway and called: "Anybody home?"

"Damn right," a voice said, and a moment later a
big, hearty man in his early forties came up from the
foc'sle stairway and stepped on deck.

"Hello, Walt," the man said, and held out a huge
hand.

"Hello, Fred," Pap said. "These are my sons: Wayne,
Duke, and this beanpole we call the Dutchman. Boys,
meet Fred Manly."

We shook hands with Fred, and I studied him. He was about six-two, powerfully built, with brown hair and piercing blue eyes. He was dressed in a heavy wool shirt and trousers, with black wool underwear showing from beneath the open neck of his shirt. A year later this big man was to save my life.

Fred said, "Come down and have breakfast."

"We've just eaten, thanks," Pap answered.

"Well, coffee then," Fred insisted, and led the way below where he introduced us to his partner, Cliff Kilkenny. Cliff was a dumpy little Irishman in his sixties. He was busy frying bacon, and watching a pan of biscuits in the oven. He poured coffee for us, then broke eight eggs into a skillet. When the bacon was done he sliced a whole liver that lay in a pan on the table, floured the slices and dropped them into the smoking skillet. I was wondering if he had heard Pap tell Fred we had already eaten. Pap must have been thinking the same thing, for he said, "We've eaten, Cliff—don't fix anything for us."

Fred laughed. "We always eat this way, Walt. We're just hogs, I guess."

Cliff finished cooking and both men piled their plates high with bacon, liver, fried eggs and biscuits—and dove in. Not a word was said as they ate, refilled their plates, and went on eating. We watched in fascination until the food was at last gone.

They stacked their dishes in the sink, then refilled

the coffee mugs and lit cigarettes. "That was seal liver," Fred said. "Best liver in the world. Cliff and me have been hunting seal for the bounty these past two months. What's our tally, Cliff?"

Cliff took a small notebook from the shelf over his bunk, and studied it. "Nine hundred and twenty-four."

"How much do you get for them?" I asked.

"Well, we get three dollars a scalp, and we can sell a few of the best skins, but there's not much demand for them."

"What's the bounty for?" Duke asked.

"They hang around the rivers and bays and feed on the spawning salmon. Until a few years ago they weren't hunted except for food by the Indians. And now there are so many that the Fish and Wildlife Service pays a bounty to keep them under control. There used to be a bounty on bald eagles too, but the old women down in the States got to whining about us shooting the national emblem and all, so they take off the bounty every now and then. They put it back again when there gets to be too many. There's a bounty on Dolly Varden trout, too. I think it's about nine cents a pound now. The Dollys hang around the salmon streams and eat the salmon eggs."

Dutch, who had never had a serious thought in his life that wasn't connected with hunting or trapping or fishing, looked at Fred, and said, "Looks to me like a person could make a living just bounty hunting."

"I believe he could," Fred agreed. "Cliff and me just

do a little hunting in the winter and spring when it's off-season for us. We're all through for this year; be starting to get the fishing gear on now."

I asked Fred how they hunted the seals, and he said that he and Cliff took the *Chester L* up into the heads of glacial inlets and anchored it. Then they set out with the skiff and outboard motor. Once they found a spot where seals were numerous, Cliff Kilkenny went ashore with his special rifle and shooting pillow and began shooting. Fred picked up the seals with the skiff. About forty per cent were "sinkers," they estimated. "If it wasn't for the ones that sink before I can get to them, we'd really have made a pile this spring," Fred said. "Show the boys your seal rifle, Cliff."

Cliff went to a rack over his bunk and took down his rifle; it was a monstrous thing with a bull-barrel, set trigger, and a huge telescope mounted over the barrel. "It's a .220 Swift," Cliff said. "Weighs almost twenty pounds. I had it made up special in the States. With everything, it cost me a little over four hundred dollars."

"Cliff can knock the eye right out of an eagle at three hundred and fifty yards," Fred said.

We talked of hunting for a little longer, then Fred asked, "When do you want to leave town, Walt?"

"Whenever you're ready," Pap answered.

"How about leaving around three this afternoon?"

"That's fine," Pap said, and we thanked the two men for the coffee and stepped out onto the float.

We had plenty to do. We would have to run the

Resolute over to the oil dock and fill its gas tanks. Groceries would have to be ordered and delivered to the steamer dock for us to pick up.

By two-thirty we had everything aboard the *Resolute*. Then Fred Manly moved the *Chester L* over to the steamer dock and we loaded bedsprings and mattresses as well as a wood-burning cook stove into the hold. Pap had bought a six-month supply of groceries uptown, and all this went into the hold also.

It was three-thirty by the time we finally had everything aboard. We decided Ma and Dutch would go aboard the *Chester L*, while Pap, Duke, and I followed in the *Resolute*. Old Spot would go with us. Before leaving, Fred studied the clouds, noting their direction and approximate speed. (This was something we all learned to do soon, for the weather reports on the radio were undependable much of the time concerning these inside passages.) "A little southeast," Fred said. "We might take some rolling out in the Sound. Anyone get seasick?"

Ma's face turned green, and she admitted that she had been sick most of the way up from Seattle, even though it had been perfect weather.

Fred Manly assured her there were always harbors in this country, and if the sea got very rough we'd go anchor up until it quieted down.

Since Fred had a few last-minute errands to run, he

told us to head on out in the *Resolute*. The *Chester L* was a much faster vessel, and he would catch up with us later. Duke and I untied the lines and got aboard; Pap, at the wheel, backed the *Resolute* away from the float and headed out the channel. The ebb tide was with us and we went whizzing past the black buoy. Watching the scattered houses on the shore, I could tell we were really moving.

As we came up on the last entrance buoy it began to get rough; there were big whirlpools in the water that sometimes caught the little *Resolute* and turned us almost completely around before Pap could get it straightened out. The farther we went the worse it seemed to get. Pap was plainly worried, and although I had spent three years in the Navy, I didn't know the first thing about small boats, so I was of little help. Finally, Pap said, "I think maybe we'd better turn around and go back to the harbor."

I thought we should too, but when we came about we soon found that we could *not* get back into the harbor. We did not know it then, of course, but what had happened was that in these inside waters the tides sometimes reach a height of twenty-one feet. This means that twenty-one feet of water has to move through the narrow channel in six hours. Consequently, we had been making approximately twelve knots going out with the ebb tide, when our actual cruising speed was something like five knots. Now when we turned and tried to get back into the Narrows, we were bucking a seven-knot current. And, in our ignorance, we stayed there and futilely fought the strong ebb tide and continued to lose ground.

Finally we saw the *Chester L* headed down the channel toward us. Fred went on by us with a nonchalant wave. We felt like a bunch of hillbillies caught gawking at a Fifth Avenue skyscraper, and Pap wheeled the cowardly *Resolute* around and took up station behind the *Chester L.*

Ma was standing on the rolling back deck of the *Chester,* looking forlornly back at the scattered houses of Petersburg as she clung to the bulwarks. I knew what she was thinking. When Pap conned her into selling our place in Oregon and moving to Alaska, he had told her that we would be only a few miles out of town, that we would be so close, in fact, we could run the *Resolute* in for a movie at night, if we so desired. As it turned out Ma didn't see a town but once in the next seven years.

The wind hit us soon after we made our turn around the last buoy and the farther out into the sound we traveled, the worse the swell became. It came on us from the starboard quarter, and the double-ended *Resolute* rolled abominably. Old Spot, sitting resignedly on the back deck, soon became seasick, and this was all Duke needed to set him heaving *his* lunch over the side. Pap and I were worried about Ma on the badly rolling *Chester L* ahead. It got worse by degrees, until one had to hang on to keep from being thrown against the sides of the cabin.

The *Chester L* plowed onward, however, and there was nothing to do but follow. While Pap steered, I got out the chart and found our position. I also put the bow on the left tangent of Sukoi Island ahead, and with the parallel rulers found that our compass was over thirty degrees in error. I decided that when we anchored for the night I'd try to adjust it.

The size of the sea continued to increase, and as we came abeam of Sukoi Island light, the *Chester L* slowed and turned in toward a small cove on the lee side. Fred dropped the anchor and we came alongside and tied to them.

"The tides are big now—almost twenty feet—that's why it's so nasty. I think we'll just wait here until slack water this evening; it'll smooth out a lot then, and we'll mosey along to Portage Bay and anchor for the night."

Dutch hadn't been sick, but Ma was in terrible shape, and I thought her condition was what had prompted Fred to stop for a while. She soon began to feel better, however, now that the boats were on an even keel; but when Cliff Kilkenny began cooking supper the smell of food drove her up on deck.

We ate an early supper, and when the tide began to slack at five-thirty, I saw Fred knew what he was talking about: the sea had gone flat, with only a little southerly chop. It would not be bad going now, so we pulled anchor and were soon on our way once more. The sky was overcast and darkness came early. Ahead, the *Chester*'s mast light went on, and so we switched on the *Resolute*'s running lights.

We had seen a few icebergs earlier, but at some distance. Now we began to run among them. In the poor light they were sometimes difficult to see. Fred had told us they broke off of the faces of the glaciers on the mainland and drifted out into the sounds and straits with the wind and tide. Off Cape Strait we suddenly hit a small one, evidently submerged, for we hadn't seen it. I immediately cut the throttle and threw the clutch into neutral; the berg bounced and grated along the metal hull of the boat. We checked the inside of the hull with a flashlight, but found no damage. Apparently it had missed the propeller, for when I engaged the clutch again the engine ran smoothly and without vibration.

It was almost ten before we saw the *Chester L* turn in toward the dark shore, and a few minutes later we began to see the Portage Bay entrance light blinking ahead. We followed the big boat through the narrow entrance, and anchored a short distance inside.

When the engine had been shut down for the night, the sudden silence was almost unbelievable. Then, imperceptibly, the night sounds began to come: the cries of gulls as they fed on a school of herring, then the sound of a whale blowing as it also moved in to feed.

Fred had two extra bunks on the *Chester L,* and after a cup of coffee Ma and Pap went below to bed. Cliff Kilkenny brought the coffee pot out on deck where we boys still sat listening to the night sounds. He refilled our cups and sat down beside us, then began to pack his pipe. Suddenly we heard a bird-like chirping not far from the side of the boat.

"What was that?" I asked.

"Land otter," Cliff said.

I became conscious of a swarm of small gnats of some kind biting me on the face and hands. They increased in density until one could hardly breathe or see, sometimes getting up the nostrils or under an eyelid.

"No-see-um's are getting too much for me, boys," Cliff said at last, "I'm going to hunt cover. See you in the morning."

We said good night, and went down into the *Resolute's* cabin, where the three of us rolled up in our sleeping bags on the foc'sle floor with Spot.

The sharp bark of a rifle awoke us the next morning, and peeking through the wheelhouse windows I saw Cliff Kilkenny lying on the deck of the *Chester* with his rifle resting on the bulwarks. As I watched he shot again at some object in the water which I was unable to see. Duke and I hurriedly dressed and went on deck.

Kilkenny rose and greeted us. He said that he'd just killed two seals, and wondered if we would be kind enough to row the skiff out to where they floated and scalp them for him. We said, "Sure," and upon receiving instruction as to the scalping we put the skiff into the water and rowed out to the dark objects in the water. When we brought the scalps back to the little Irishman, he grinned, and said: "Now tyle me, byes, where else might a mon make six dollars so easy afore breakfast?" He had something there, and I was already thinking about buying myself a bounty rifle.

After breakfast we hauled anchor and headed out into Frederick Sound once again. Four hours later we had Turnabout Island behind us, and were on the last leg of the journey. We had been traveling in the lee of Kupreanof Island, however, and as we headed across toward Admiralty Island the wind began to hit us with some force. The sea began to build up as it had the previous morning, and once more Duke and Spot were seasick (as well as Ma, I knew, aboard the *Chester L*). As the wind increased, Fred changed course, and two miserable hours later we pulled into a snug little harbor on Admiralty Island called Chapin Bay.

We lay at anchor the rest of the day, and we boys borrowed Fred's skiff and outboard motor and went seal hunting. We took six seals between us, and were quite proud of ourselves.

During the night the wind had gone down, and early the next morning we pulled anchor and ran out into Frederick Sound to find it glassy calm. We steamed onward, following the shore of Admiralty Island toward Murder Cove. Ever since our arrival in Alaska the weather had been foul, but this morning the sky was clear and the early morning sun rose from behind the mainland, coloring the icy spires of the mountain mass to the west that stretched for as far as the eye could see. Baranof Island, the chart said. It had been named for Alexander Baranof, I knew, the man who had commanded the Russian-American Company in Sitka before we had bought Alaska in 1867. I took up the binoculars and studied this impressive island that was over a hundred miles long. Snow still covered the jagged peaks, and in the valleys between them the snow piled up to such a depth that I knew it stayed there the year around. As you looked down the shore-line toward the distant ocean, each successive point and headland was a lighter shade of purple, until at last there was just a pale blur that met the sea.

With the aid of the chart we tried to identify the land around us. The mainland was over our stern, and on our starboard hand was Admiralty Island where our home would be. South of us some fourteen miles were Kuiu and Kupreanof Islands. This was sure some country.

Ahead, I saw the spout of a whale, and I pointed it out to Duke, who had never seen one. We watched and presently the huge tail arched into the air and the whale dove. A school of porpoises picked us up off Herring

Bay, and they stayed with us all the way to Murder Cove, sometimes running so close beneath the boat that we thought they would surely hit the hull or propeller, but they didn't.

Near nine o'clock we passed around Carol Island and twenty minutes later we were entering the mouth of Murder Cove. Ahead lay the sprawling red buildings of the cannery.

There was just a skeleton crew working at the cannery, but Cliff Erickson, the summer superintendent, had come in by mailboat the day before. Cliff was amazed when Pap told him that he'd moved the rest of the family to Alaska.

"But what will you do with them?" Cliff asked.

"We plan on settling in Surprise Harbor," Pap said. "We'll live in a tent until we get a log cabin up. I'll get the boys started before I begin work here, and they can finish it."

Cliff, one of the old-school Statesiders who lived in Seattle and came north every spring and left in the fall, was stunned. "But why on earth would anyone want to live out in the bush like this the year around! Do you have any idea of what the winters are like, Walt?"

I don't suppose Pap could have explained his desires to a city man like Cliff if he had cared to. "Don't you worry about us, Cliff," he said with finality, "we'll make out just fine."

Cliff stood looking out over Murder Cove. At last he

said, "Well, you know what you want to do, Walt . . . it will be a week before I'll need you here, why don't you and your boys wreck the old bunkhouse for the lumber—you can have it for taking it down. There's not much of a stand of cabin logs around close, and I think you might make better time with your house if you wreck the bunkhouse and use the lumber."

Pap thanked Cliff, and said he'd have a look at it. We all walked over to where it stood. The new bunkhouse had just been completed, and this old one was an eyesore, all right. But Pap said that the lumber in it was good—we could get almost everything we needed from the building, including doors and windows.

Pap asked Cliff if we could store some of our things in one of the warehouses until we were ready to move them into the new house. Cliff said, "Sure," and we went back and unloaded the things that we wouldn't need immediately and stored them.

When the *Chester L* was at last unloaded, and Fred Manly and Cliff Kilkenny were ready to leave, Pap asked Fred what he owed him. Fred just grinned. "Aw, forget it, Walt," he said. When Pap insisted, Fred said, "Heck, we had to go to town for fuel and groceries, anyway, and this is on our way to Kelp Bay. No, you keep the money, very likely you'll need it. You'll do something for us someday. . . ."

And that was it. There was definitely something different about the people in this country. Pap had figured he owed Fred around three hundred dollars for his time and use of the boat, but this man, whom he scarcely knew, had pushed it off with, *you'll do something for us someday.*

That afternoon we began wrecking the old bunkhouse. We had set up the tent on the beach nearby and Ma used a Coleman Burner to cook on. We worked fourteen hours a day, and four days later we had the building down. We carried the lumber to the beach and rafted it together, and the following day we took down the tent and put it aboard the *Resolute.* We loaded on our camping gear and tools, then borrowed a cannery skiff and set out for Surprise Harbor with the lumber raft in tow.

It was late afternoon when we finally got back into the head of Surprise Harbor. We towed the lumber raft ashore at high water (we were already learning to take advantage of the tides when possible), and then began to unload our camping equipment. While the rest of the family carried our things up the sandy beach to the edge of the woods, Dutch and I ran the *Resolute* out to deeper water and anchored it, then rowed back in the skiff.

We set up the tent near the site that Pap had picked for the house, some seventy-five yards from a small stream. It was a pretty spot. Towering spruce and hemlock and yellow cedar stood at the back of a small natural clearing, and we would not have to go far for firewood. Surprise Harbor was open to the south, and in the distance, across Chatham Strait, the magnificent Baranof Island rose like a picture postcard of the Alps to dominate our view.

When we had things shipshape, Ma sent Dutch to the creek for a bucket of water and then began cooking supper. Pap, never idle, took a shovel out to test the soil. Soon he was back with a shovel full to show Ma. "Look, Grace, good black soil! I'll bet all we'll need will be a little lime to grow a fine garden."

We built a fire in front of the tent, and were sitting there waiting for supper, when Pap stood up and said softly, "Look yonder, boys . . . a fine buck!" We turned to follow his pointing finger and saw a three-pointer walking slowly along the creek bank. Dutch ran to get his rifle, but Pap stopped him with a curt word. "We just as well get something settled right now! We've moved into a virgin country that's seldom if ever been hunted, and there is an abundance of game, but I will not tolerate you boys killing anything just for the sake of killing. That deer, now, lives out his life within four or five miles of the place where he was born. He'll be around this fall, and the fall after that . . . we'll get him when he's prime, but we will not *ever* shoot an animal that's in poor shape." Pap paused to roll and light a cigarette, then went on, "Think of this country as our private storehouse for food"—he waved a hand to encompass all of Surprise Harbor and the ridges and mountains behind. "We'll not worry about the game laws or the limits prescribed, but we'll have our own set of laws. I'd say, offhand, deer will be in good shape somewhere near the middle of August, and except for rutting season, we'll probably take them up into December. And we'll watch out for them; in the winters when the heavy snow drives them to the beaches to starve, we'll cut down cedar trees for them to feed on." He finished the cigarette and tossed it into the fire, and was silent for a long time. When he spoke again he had what he wanted to say pretty well thought out. "We're going to be here a long time, boys . . . and after I'm gone there will be your sons and their sons to think of. I'd hate like hell to think of the day when a man couldn't go out and get a piece of meat."

After supper Dutch and I took our rifles and, calling Spot, followed the creek back into the timber. Near a bend in the creek Spot began barking excitedly. Dutch and I ran ahead just in time to see a huge brown bear go into the brush. We found the bear's tracks in the soft sand of the creek, and a pile of steaming manure. When Dutch and I returned to camp we told the others of seeing the bear.

We were up the next morning before daylight, and Ma began breakfast. When we had eaten, she sent Dutch to the creek for water to wash the dishes, and the rest of us went to work sawing yellow cedar for foundation blocks. We had been working only a few minutes when we heard old Spot raising a racket in the elder thicket of the creek. Then, as we waited undecided, there came the dull bark of Dutch's .25/20. We all ran for our rifles in the tent, and raced for the creek.

There beside the pool where we dipped our drinking water lay a huge brownie, and over against the far bank Dutch was hunched over Spot who bled from a deep gash along his back.

The brownie had strolled out of the woods just as Dutch was filling his water bucket, and Spot, without a moment's hesitation, had gone straight for the intruder. During the melee, Dutch managed to grab his old relic of a rifle which he had left on the creek bank, and waited for an opening.

The lack of Spot's right-hind leg—the result of a duel with a mowing machine some years previous—made it difficult for him to keep clear of the brownie's slashing attack. One huge paw caught him along the back, and Dutch, desperate now, had made a fast snapshot at the bear's head. Luck was with him that morning, for the puny bullet caught the huge animal squarely in the ear. Down it had gone, killed instantly by a rifle we later discarded because it wasn't *skookum* enough for deer hunting.

"Boys," Pap said, shaken by the size of the brownie, "we've got to be mighty careful of these bears from now on!"

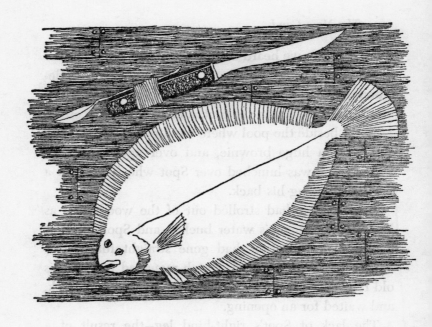

3
GREENHORN FISHERMEN

From the moment we began driving tent stakes until
at last we finished the cabin we were to live in, we
constantly fought against time. Four days after we
towed the lumber raft ashore in the head of Surprise

Harbor we had the foundation finished, stringers, floor joists, and floor in place, the wall studs up and ready for the ceiling joists and rafters.

On the fifth morning Pap was to begin work at the cannery, and after an early breakfast he set off along the trail we had blazed across the peninsula to Murder Cove, a half-hour walk away. The peninsula, which separated Surprise Harbor from Murder Cove, was approximately two miles long. We had purchased an old skiff from the cannery, and we left it moored there on the west side of Murder Cove and used it to cross to the cannery on the opposite shore. In the late 1860's, shortly after the United States purchased Alaska, the Thlinget Indians, from Saginaw Bay on Kuiu Island, had murdered two white prospectors at Tyee—and so the little bay was known thereafter as Murder Cove. Before that, the Russians had used it briefly for a slave camp; a whaling station had operated there in the early part of the twentieth century; finally, it changed hands and a pioneering fishing family had started a salmon cannery. In the twenties, the firm of Sebastian and Stuart of Seattle purchased the small cannery, rebuilt and expanded its operation, and continued to process fish.

With Pap working at the cannery, the finishing of the cabin was left to us boys and Ma, who could handle a hammer and saw like the veteran she was. We worked hard those days, because there was much to be done even after the cabin was finished. A woodshed would have to be built, trees felled, sawed and split, and an outside toilet erected. A garden spot had to be cleared and spaded, for Ma was anxious to begin planting the seeds she had brought from the States.

We worked from daylight to dark on the house, with Pap's help on Sundays, and, eight days after we had started the foundation, we were ready to move in. We set up the wood-burning cook stove, hastily built a table, benches, cupboards, and we were in business. The cabin was twenty by thirty feet, and the front half of it served as kitchen, living and dining rooms. There were two bedrooms in the rear.

Since Dutch had killed the big brownie at the creek we were hard pressed to keep him at work. Duke and I tried everything we could think of to keep him busy, but soon he'd get that faraway look in his eyes and presently we'd discover he was gone, off somewhere in the woods to trail bears, or up on the high ridges looking for deer sign. He paid little attention to my orders to keep working, and, since Duke was more his age, I'd get him to take Dutch out in the brush and pound some discipline into him. But Dutch was indifferent to this treatment, and the next day he'd be off again, rifle in hand, old Spot limping along behind as he wandered through the forest.

At last we hit upon a plan to keep Dutch at work. It was relatively simple. Dutch had long been fascinated

by games of chance, so I took him aside one morning and told him if he'd really get in and work I'd pay
him a dollar an hour out of my own money. As we sus-
pected he quickly fell for this line, for the wheels turned
and he began to visualize the rifles, ammunition, and
traps he could buy with this big money.

At the end of the first day I paid Dutch off—twelve
dollars in cash. That evening after supper was over, I
took a pair of trick dice out of my seabag, a pair I'd
bought from a novelty store when I was in the Navy.
Without even so much as glancing at the Dutchman, I
casually asked Duke if he'd like to shoot a little craps;
he said he would. After watching us a few minutes,
Dutch asked if he could play. In a very short time I had
my twelve dollars back, and had loaned Dutch money
against his next day's wages. Dutch proved to be a
compulsive gambler and, like the old southern land-
owners, I kept him thereafter in debt to me; the only
way he could hope to get clear of his obligations was
to saw more firewood. And at night Duke and I would
take it away from him again in our game of chance.

Ma thought that this was a pretty dirty trick for us
to play on our own brother, but when I asked her how
else we could keep him working, she didn't know.

Finally we were finished. We left Ma planting her
garden, and moved the *Resolute* around the peninsula
to the cannery dock in Murder Cove to finish rigging it
for fishing. A good many other trolling boats were

rigging out at the float there, getting ready for the halibut season which opened the first of May. We had only a vague idea of how to rig a commercial troller, and we hung around the other boats hoping some of the fishermen would offer some information. One of the first things we learned, however, was that about ninety per cent of the fishermen were Scandinavians—and a very clannish lot indeed. Our questions were not answered with much grace, for we were *cheechakoes*—greenhorns, Johnny-come-latelys. Their attitude was clearly this: Why should we tell you the things it has taken us years to learn the hard way? Why should we go out of our way to help you, then have you out on the fishing grounds competing with us?

We went ahead with the rigging as best we could. We did the things we understood, like cutting twenty-five-foot spruce poles, peeling and then mounting them on either side of the *Resolute*'s cabin on hinged strap irons so they might be lowered to forty-five-degree angles when we fished. Most of the larger boats used four poles; two "bow" poles, and two "main" poles amidship. We had decided that we would fish only two poles since the *Resolute* did not appear to be long enough to fish four lines without tangling. On the larger boats, forty-pound lead sinkers were used on the bow lines, twenty-pounders on the main lines. I thought thirty-pound leads might be about right for us.

But still so many, many things escaped us. I knew

that our stainless-steel wire ran from the gurdies (small bronze power drums which held the wires) through overhead blocks, and that the "cannon balls," or lead sinkers, were attached to the ends. I had also learned that, about every four fathoms along the wire, the fishermen half-hitched linen twine "markers" into which the leaders were snapped, and that these markers not only kept the leaders from slipping up and down the lines, but served also to let you know how deep you were fishing. But what I couldn't understand was how you got the line out to the ends of the poles to catch the fish—then back again to the side of the boat when you landed one.

We would probably still be trying to figure it out if Paul Stromgren hadn't taken pity upon us. We had met Paul when first we came to Murder Cove. He and his wife, Jerry, wintered there. Paul was about five-eight, slender, in his late forties. He was a Canadian by birth, and a mixture of Norwegian and English. I believe he was the most even-tempered man I have ever known. Some years later when he was then living in Jim Petersen's Cove, perhaps a mile east of the cannery, his boat was found half sunk at its mooring near the cannery. The watchman became excited and sent a fisherman who happened to be tied to the dock at the time over the trail to Paul's cabin. The man ran all the way and arrived out of breath and on the verge of collapse just as Paul was sitting down to breakfast.

"Paul," he gasped, "your boat is sinking!"

"Oh!" Paul said, and invited the man to have breakfast with them.

"*I said your boat is sinking!*" the man shouted.

"Good riddance," Paul said matter-of-factly. "Now sit down, Nick, and eat a good breakfast—you're in terrible shape." They had breakfast, another cup of coffee; Paul lit a cigar, then looked at the tide book. High tide would be at eleven-thirty A.M. Paul proposed a pinochle game; and at ten o'clock he and Nick put on their coats and walked back toward the cannery.

The boat would have sunk, Paul had realized, before they could possibly have got to it. The water where the boat had been moored was only four fathoms deep and now, with high tide, he could get a line onto the mast and tow it ashore. When the tide went out he would simply bore a hole in the bottom to drain it; then he could overhaul the engine and repair the leak in the hull at his leisure. It was not anything to get excited about.

A good many interesting stories could be written of people who have migrated to Alaska, but Paul's life always has fascinated me. It spoke of adventure, and of the what-the-hell attitude of the depression years.

Paul, in his wanderings from one job to another, found himself in Los Angeles one day in the mid-thirties. He was a good all-around workman, carpenter, plasterer; he could hang paper, or repair an automobile engine, and so had little difficulty finding a job. He was single, and with money coming in he had enough to do him. He made friends easily, and soon knew most of the local bootleggers.

As the depression worsened, however, the contractor he worked for laid him off reluctantly so that a man with a family might work. He was unable to find another job, and one evening at a party he met a man his own age known as Conn. They took an instant liking to each other, talked of the economic situation, and wondered what was left for them to do. When the party ran out of booze, Paul and Conn volunteered to drive over to the bootlegger's for more; by the time they returned, they had decided to combine their assets and head north. It did not matter where they were going—just that they were leaving town.

The next day they sold Conn's car, packed their belongings in Paul's Ford, and drove north. In Seattle they found themselves on the waterfront looking at boats. They soon found one for sale and, throwing together every dime they possessed, were able to purchase it. It was thirty-two feet long, powered with a Model-T Ford engine. Paul sold his car in order to fill the gasoline tanks and two fifty-gallon drums on deck. The remaining money went for groceries—the bulk of which was a hundred-pound sack of rice and a hundred-pound sack of red beans. Paul reasoned that with this reserve they were not likely to starve. They stowed their possessions, and on a fine summer day cast loose their lines and headed north. Between them they had exactly fifty cents—just before leaving they had discovered they had two sets of oars for the skiff, and since it is bad luck to begin a long journey dead broke, they had sold them to the man tied next to them for this amount.

They still had no idea of where they were going, but this didn't worry them. They took their time, enjoying the fine weather and the beauty of their trip up the Inside Passage.

Every little bay and inlet seemed to beckon and, before they knew it, it was September and still they were not out of Canada. At last they crossed into Alaska, stopping briefly at Ketchikan, then Wrangell and Petersburg. Coming across Frederick Sound they finally ran into trouble. The oil pan on the engine had rusted through and sprung a leak, and they did not notice it until the engine froze up solid.

Paul rigged a makeshift sail and, with Conn pulling the skiff, they managed to tow the boat into a small harbor not far from Murder Cove. It was named Bensen Cove, and Paul was to spend the best part of his life within a few miles of this spot where, by circumstances, they were compelled to land.

They anchored that night, and the next morning examined the ancient Model-T engine. It was clearly beyond repair. As they sat there debating what to do, a sudden snowstorm quickly decided for them. It was November, and the frigid breath of winter was in the air. Bensen Cove was open to southeasterly storms and they would not be able to keep the boat anchored there.

The following day they built a cradle from drift logs on the beach, and rigged a homemade windlass to pull the boat and cradle above the high-tide mark. Then they began cutting logs for a cabin. Winter had set in before they finished, but it was a happy day when at last they were able to move into their new home. Although they had eaten most of their canned food, the hundred-pound sacks of rice and beans were barely touched. Deer, ducks, and geese were plentiful—and they had rifles and a shotgun. There was also a good clam bed in front of the cabin, so they had no worry about food. They were most distressed about being out of tobacco, but perhaps one of these days they would walk over to the cannery in Murder Cove and buy some with their hoarded fifty-cent piece. . . .

So now, as we tried to get the *Resolute* ready to fish, it was a real pleasure to have Paul there to help us out. And it was the beginning of a deep friendship with this extraordinary man.

"Well," Paul said, after looking at the mess we had made of rigging out the *Resolute,* "if I were you, I think I'd tear off most of this and start over. Here's the proper way to do it. . . ."

Slowly, day by day, we began to get the *Resolute* shipshape. There were many things to be learned out on the grounds, but now at least we were rigged out properly. And whenever we thought of something we would like to know more about, we would walk over to Paul's boat; Jerry would put on the ever-present coffee pot while Paul explained such-and-such a thing.

At last we were ready, and when the halibut season opened on May first we started up the engine and steamed out of the harbor entrance full of enthusiasm. But it was short-lived, for we soon ran into difficulties even Paul couldn't help us with. Paul was one of the elite—strictly a king-salmon troller who would not stoop to fish halibut. He continued to lie at the float in Murder Cove until the king salmon began to show in June. We were lost without him. Although we had charts of the area around Tyee, they proved to give only a general idea of the depth and bottom contour. And one had to know the bottom intimately, as well as understand the complexities of the tide, which sometimes reached a height of twenty-one feet.

On our first day out we were utterly whipped. We followed some of the larger boats out to the grounds, but no sooner had we put out our gear than the strong flood tide drifted us onto a rocky underwater pinnacle and stripped off both lines and the leads and lures—everything went.

There was nothing to do but run back to the cannery

and buy more gear. It cost seventy dollars to replace what had been lost, and we were terribly discouraged. "There's more to this fishing than meets the eye, I guess," Duke said. I was too disappointed even to answer.

We rolled the new stainless-steel lines onto the gurdy drums, attached the heavy lead sinkers, and went forth the following day—once again to lose both lines on the mysterious underwater reef. We came in that evening to replace our lost gear again, and to watch with envy the other boats return with decks loaded with halibut. We had lost not only a hundred and forty dollars' worth of fishing gear, but also two days in which we had not caught a single fish.

That evening, after I had finished putting on new lines, I wandered to the far end of the float where the skipper of the *Pauline*, a short, powerfully built man named Ed Wellseley, was dressing halibut. He had come to Tyee on the opening day of the season, and he was acknowledged the high-liner of the fishing fleet. When I asked how much fish he had, he said somewhere around three thousand pounds, he thought. At seventeen cents a pound, I quickly figured that he had made over five hundred dollars that day.

Ed was a friendly individual, and when he asked how we had done, I told him of our troubles. Ed squinted his eyes thoughtfully, then called for his "boat puller" to bring him another cup of coffee. When it came, he slipped off a canvas glove saturated with fish blood and slime. He lit a cigarette, drank the cup of scalding coffee, then went back to work dressing halibut. I was fascinated. He seemed to make about three quick slashes with his long, razor-sharp knife, and then jerked gills, guts-and-all out in one easy motion. Then he reversed his knife, which had a large kitchen spoon lashed to its handle, and scraped the blood clot from the backbone of the fish. I had never seen anything else done so quickly or efficiently in my life.

"Well," Ed said at last, squinting against the cloud of cigarette smoke that rose around his face, "I think I can get you to catching halibut. Get yourself a coil of nine-thread buoy line, and a halibut anchor, then follow me out in the morning. I'll anchor you up on a good spot out there. You boys can probably do just as good jigging for them as trolling, and you won't have to worry about hanging up and losing your gear."

Duke and I promptly went up to the cannery store and bought a twelve hundred-foot coil of buoy line, and a twenty-five-pound halibut anchor. We were up early the next morning and already had eaten breakfast when we heard the *Pauline's* engine start up. We promptly started ours, and untied the lines. We moved out into the bay and waited while Ed backed away from the float and came our way. We fell in behind the *Pauline*, the throttle on our engine wide open in an effort to keep up. But our twenty-five horsepower engine was no match for the *Pauline,* and we began to fall behind. Presently Ed slowed down to let us catch up.

There was a slight swell rolling in from the southwest when we came to the fishing grounds. Ed slowed down and began jockeying, and at Ed's wave I moved the *Resolute* up alongside of him.

"We're right on the spot now!" Ed shouted. "Get yourself some landmarks!"

I looked around. To the west the light at Point Gardener fell naturally into a deep V in the mountains across on Baranof Island. I turned and faced the north and was able to line up Bartlett Point with a prominent snowslide on Admiralty. To the southeast I got a line-up over Yasha Islaid on Kuiu.

"All right," I called to Ed, "I've got a fix."

"Fine. Now, listen: you can only fish the flood tide here. It's just beginning to flood now, and the tide runs in this direction." He pointed. "Now, to end up over this gut where the fish are, you must drop your anchor about two hundred yards ahead. Come on."

We moved slowly ahead; Duke was at the wheel, Dutch and I were on the bow with the anchor gear ready.

"All right, let her go!" Ed yelled.

"Throw it over, Dutch," I said, and took a quick fix, for I wanted to be able to drop the anchor in exactly the same spot again.

"Your anchor is in fifty-six fathoms of water," Ed

called. "When you drift back over the gut you'll be in forty-three fathoms. The fish are right on the bottom. Use nothing but herring until you catch some cod, then chop them up for bait. Cod stay on the hooks better than herring. Okay?"

"Okay, Ed," I said. "And thanks!"

Ed stepped back to the *Pauline's* cockpit and began to get his own gear ready.

The tide was still taking us along, and Dutch was paying out line from the coil on our bow. As my landmarks began to come into sight we took a strain on the anchor and made the line fast to the cleat. We were right on the money, according to my landmarks. I just hoped Ed knew what he was talking about and that we were over halibut.

We all went back to the cockpit and let the heavy lead sinkers over the side. While Duke and I snapped several short leaders on just above the sinker, Dutch broke open a fifty-pound block of frozen herring and began cutting them in two. We baited our hooks and let them down slowly to the bottom, forty-odd fathoms below us. With one hand resting on the stainless-steel line, we waited for bites.

A few minutes later Duke said, "I think I've got something on."

I moved over to his side and felt his line. Something sure was romping around down there. Ed had told us to let it "soak" for a while, even if we did feel fish on,

and give it a chance to "load up." We waited as long
as we could contain ourselves, then Duke threw in the
clutch to the power gurdy and began to bring up the
line. About the same time I felt a few tentative tugs
on my line, then a hard pull. Soon the line was jerking
steadily.

We were all hanging over the water on Duke's side
as the first of the leaders neared the surface. Suddenly
white bellies flashed from deep beneath the water as the
halibut twisted and fought to free themselves. We were
using five leaders, and we had five halibut! As the first
leader broke water, Duke unsnapped it, and beat the
fish unmercifully with the back side of the gaff-hook.
(The gaff is usually a small club, sometimes a junior-
size baseball bat, with a large steel hook set in the end
of it.) Duke sunk the hook in the halibut's head and
jerked it aboard. Dutch, on deck with another hook,
slid the flopping fish into the big wooden fish box. I
judged the halibut to weigh perhaps forty pounds. We
were elated.

While Duke unloaded his line and rebaited his hooks,
I began to bring up the line on my side. I had four
halibut, and a grey cod, which Dutch butchered and
chopped into bait for us. From then on, until the tide
began the change six hours later, we were busy, and
soon the fish box on deck was filled to overflowing. We
all whooped and laughed whenever we brought up a
line loaded with fish; we had quickly forgotten the two

previous days of bad luck. A few scraps of boards were left and Dutch got the saw and hammer and nailed together a makeshift fish bin to hold the flopping halibut.

Halibut are strange creatures. Much like the enigmatic salmon, who disappear into the ocean not to be seen until they again return at the end of their cycle to spawn, the halibut move out in the deep in the winters, then back to shallower ground in the spring. Their size varies greatly—from six-pounders (the smallest that legally may be kept) to giant four-hundred-odd pounders. Both sexes have "testicles," though the largest halibut are reputed to be the females. And a mature halibut is long-lived; the people who should know estimate their lifespan to be comparable to man's.

The largest any of us have caught was taken by Pap the following summer, and dressed out at 360 pounds; it was over nine feet long. Pap shot it with a rifle and towed it around until he could attract the attention of Dutch who was fishing nearby in a skiff. They had to rig a block-and-tackle in order to get it aboard.

When the tide at last began to change the halibut quit biting, as if by signal, and we straightened our aching backs and began the chore of pulling the anchor line out of the depths by hand. But we felt good, for we estimated we had somewhere near eleven hunded pounds for the day—possibly one hundred and fifty dollars' worth of dressed fish.

When we had the anchor aboard, we ran back into

Murder Cove and tied to the float to dress our halibut. Until now we had been concerned only with catching them. It had never occurred to us that there might be a trick to dressing them. I tried it first. Selecting a fish from one of the bins, I sharpened the big, long-bladed dressing knife, and went to work. When I was through there seemed to be more guts and gills still clinging to the fish than I had taken out. It had taken me approximately twenty minutes to dress the halibut, and looking at the half-ton or more of fish in the bins, I began to realize that we might be there all night. Duke tried his hand with the next one, but he was just as slow and awkward as I had been.

We were still at it when the sun went down. The other fishermen had long since sold their catch, and occasionally one of them would stop a moment to watch us, then go back to his boat chuckling at our efforts. There was nothing funny about it to us, for the dreaded no-see-ums had come out now that the sun was down, and they drove us crazy as we tried to clean fish and brush them away at the same time.

Finally Ed Wellseley stopped by. He shook his head sadly as he watched our efforts. "Let me show you how to dress a halibut, boys," he said, and climbed into the cockpit beside me. I gladly relinquished the knife.

"They practically clean themselves," Ed said. "You sever the throat-latch like this. Then make a cut on each side of the gills, rip open the belly to the vent, a touch of the knife point here, there—then a jerk of the gills brings the whole works out. Simple, huh? Now, take the second finger of your right hand and run it up beneath the membrane of this blood clot on the backbone. Take out the testicles, then scrape out the blood clot, as well as this sweet-meat in the throat since that's what spoils first. Got it?"

I nodded as Ed climbed out of the cockpit, but I was mentally going over all the intricate steps he'd just shown me before I'd forget them.

In due time we learned to clean a thousand pounds an hour—*apiece*! But right now we were overwhelmed by the many facets of this fascinating business. We woke each morning full of excitement, as we wondered what the new day would bring.

Ed Wellseley was the high-liner of the fleet, and our idol. Of course there were many fishermen who didn't like him; people seldom like a man who constantly outdoes them. But you could not find a friend more loyal than Ed. And over the years there is seldom a season goes by that Ed is not showing the ropes to some *cheechako*.

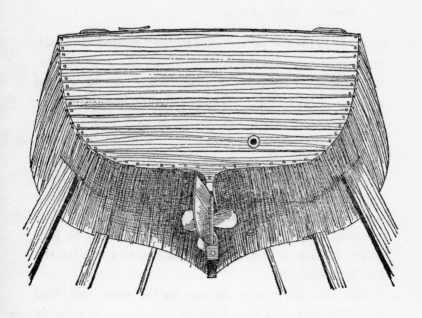

4
PAP BUYS A BOAT

We were doing well by fishing the same spot where Ed had told us to anchor. The halibut were nice-sized—twenty to sixty pounds. Although two lines were all we were able to use without tangling on the *Resolute,* we decided to tie the skiff some fifty feet behind the boat, and one of us could fish from it with a cotton hand line. Dutch tried it first, and it worked fine. At the end of the day he had yarded up over four hundred pounds of halibut out of the depths. His hands were blistered and sore, but he had made almost sixty dollars! From then on each of us took a turn in the skiff every third day, and between the *Resolute* and skiff managed to average between seven hundred fifty and a thousand pounds of fish a day. We paid all expenses: gasoline and oil, bait, fishing gear—and the net was split four ways: a share to each of us, and a share to Pap for the use of the *Resolute*.

This was big money to me; to the boys, who had picked berries and hops back in Oregon for practically nothing, it was almost unbelievable. Every time one of us brought up a line of fish, Dutch would yell, "We're sure making it big, huh? What are you going to do with your share, Duke?"

"I'm gonna buy me the fanciest custom-made bounty rifle that you've even see. What you gonna get?"

And so the talk would go all day long. Sometimes the sea would be rough, and Duke would be seasick. Sometimes the wind and rain lashed at us for days on end, but we were making money and we fished until the weather finally drove us into the harbor.

Every night, after we finished dressing our fish, we moved the boat over to the fish hoist and sold our catch

to Honest John, the fish buyer. We'd take our ticket up to the company office and cash it, then head for home. Most of the time it would be close to midnight before we got there, but Ma always had supper waiting. As we came to the creek, Duke and Dutch would forget their weariness and race to the house to tell Ma and Pap how well we had done that day.

Next morning we would be up before daylight, wash and eat, then strike out along the trail to Murder Cove, still sleepy and stiff and sore, but looking eagerly forward to the new day.

And this first flush of success was to have a profound effect on Dutch and me; it started a way of life to which we became slaves. Bad years were to come, years in which we would barely pay for the expense of operating a boat, but we endured these, for always in the back of our minds were thoughts of the big money—*the four- and five-hundred-dollar days!*

Duke was of a different temperament; he liked the good days fine, but he could not take the poor days when we might put in eighteen hours and not catch a single fish. Ma used to say that she could tell what kind of a day we'd had by looking at Duke's face when we crossed the creek at night. The next year Duke was to leave fishing and go to work at the cannery.

The halibut season lasted through May, and when we totaled up our receipts we found that we had taken in thirty-eight hundred dollars. Even with all expenses out we each had around eight hundred and fifty. Pap's share for the use of the boat was more than twice the amount he had earned at the cannery during the same time. Even Ma was impressed.

With the end of the halibut season, we began to rig out for king salmon. Here we were again, going into something new, into another phase of commercial fishing that we knew nothing of. But we had Paul to help us once more, and we would learn as had others before us. We had one thing in our favor, however: during the month that we fished halibut, we had learned the direction in which the different stages of the tide ran, and it was not long before we came to know the Tyee area fairly well.

Dutch had been anxious to have a boat of his own and, when the halibut season closed, he bought a sixteen-foot, round-bottomed skiff from a Thlinget Indian who worked at the cannery. He ordered a five-horsepower outboard motor from town, and began to troll with hand lines for king salmon. Dutch was a born "mountain man"; in the years ahead he never made a dime in any way except from fishing, trapping, or bounty hunting.

Trolling for salmon is perhaps the most frustrating of occupations. You can be fishing right alongside another boat, dragging exactly the same kind of gear as the other man—yet he will catch fish and you won't. You increase your speed, decrease it, move all around the other boat—and still you can't get them to bite. This can go on for days at a time. Or weeks. Steve Irwin on the *Sea Hog* once went six weeks without catching a fish of any kind. All of us showed him our gear and tried to help him in every way, but he still could not catch fish. Steve was at his wits end. "If only I could catch a little sea bass, or a sickly old cod, I'd feel better!" he cried one evening. A number of years ago, another fisherman was so utterly beaten by a long streak of bad luck, that finally he went berserk, and ran his boat full speed onto the rocky beach near where he was fishing. He grabbed a shotgun and a box of shells, waded ashore and began shooting at his boat which, ironically enough, was named *Good Fortune*. When his fishermen friends came close to pick him up, he shot at them, too.

One day in mid-August a heavy timber fell on Pap while he and the head carpenter at the cannery were repairing a portion of the dock. The blow knocked him unconscious and the crew carried him up to the office for first-aid.

When Pap finally regained consciousness, he sat up and rubbed his head, and someone lit a cigarette for him. After his head had cleared, he looked at Cliff Ericson and said: "Write out my time, Cliff. This is my last job."

Cliff urged him to reconsider, or at least sleep on it, but Pap stood by his guns, and when we all came home from fishing that evening he was waiting for us. After selling the day's catch and washing down the *Resolute*, we all rowed across the bay and walked the trail home to Surprise Harbor.

Pap broke out a hidden bottle of brandy, and after supper we drank to the future. When Ma asked him what he would do, Pap said, "I know where I can buy a boat for a thousand dollars. Needs a new engine, and some work, but it should make a pretty fair troller. We need something larger, anyway, something we can pack ice with and cover more country like the other boats do. When there's poor fishing here at Tyee, we'll be able to move to where there are fish."

The next day we rowed out to see Happy Dave, on the *Vanguard*, which was anchored in the lee of Deer Island.

When you come right down to it, this country is populated by "misfits"—those of us who are unable to accept the conventional way of life. Most of us work a great deal harder to survive out in the wilderness than we would if we had safe nine-to-five jobs in the city, but we would be miserable with such an existence. There are many kinds of misfits, from the hard-working ones to the near-bums who live out in a tent or shack or derelict boat with the barest essentials.

Happy Dave was one of the latter. He was a veteran of World War One who had been gassed in France, and his legs were covered by shrapnel scars. But Dave was quick to point out that he was not bothered much by this. "I'm sorry that I can't use the war as an excuse as to the way I live. No, I'm just a bum at heart, boys." On work he'd say, "I just can't stand the smell of sweat—my own." On his drinking habits, "I haven't got the will power of a chicken."

After the war Dave had gone to work as a game warden in the Alaska Game Commission, but he just didn't have the heart to run in an offender who, if he had any imagination at all, could easily touch Dave's sympathetic spot. He soon lost this job and drifted from one thing to another. His longest one was bootlegging during prohibition. This required a minimum of work, provided refreshments, and his product was always in demand. Dave once told me that after taking a load of moonshine to Warm Springs Bay, he returned to his hide-out and found an Indian lying dead in front of his still, a tin cup still in his hand. When I asked Dave what he did, he said, "Why, I moved the still, of course!"

As Happy Dave grew older, and legal whisky came back, money was more difficult to come by. He lived out in remote spots, alone, existing mainly on venison and clams, trapping enough to buy a few staples—and to go on a "toot" every now and then. In 1945 he made one last effort to get a little stake, and took a job as cook and deckhand on the mailboat *Yakobi* running out of Juneau. He told Martin Fisk, the owner, to hold his wages for him until he had enough to buy a fishing boat.

By spring Martin had saved enough for Dave to buy the *Vanguard*, a thirty-two-foot derelict reputed to be one of the oldest vessels still afloat in Alaska. Now that Dave had a mobile home, he roamed around the country during the summer and tied the boat to some isolated cannery dock in the winter. On rare occasions he even fished a little.

When we first moved to Surprise Harbor, the *Vanguard* was anchored behind Deer Island, a mile or so from where we built the house. Happy Dave made sporadic attempts to get out to the fishing grounds, but being a master at evading actual labor he usually had enough excuses to keep the anchor down. He would set his herring net out in the bay for bait, for he belonged to the old school and had little faith in those new-fangled spoons and plugs; fresh herring was the *only* thing to catch king salmon with. But after picking the herring from the net he'd have to take the rest of the day off to relax. The next day the weather would not look so good; the clouds were moving too fast . . . maybe tomorrow it would be better. By the third day the herring would be half-rotten, and everyone knows that you cannot "choke" herring properly when their bellies are falling out.

During the summer of 1946, Dave's total receipts from fishing amounted to exactly nine dollars and thirty-two cents. I know, because he pulled alongside me late one evening and asked if I'd take a big king salmon into the cold storage and sell it for him. It was the only fish he caught that summer. But he was happy.

He was a voracious reader, and people all over the country saved magazines for him. His favorites were *Time, Newsweek,* and *Reader's Digest,* and, although he had spent thirty years in the brush, he was as well informed on world affairs as any man I ever knew. Dave had an earthy sense of humor, much like that of Will Rogers, and could hold your attention for hours with his yarns.

Although the *Vanguard* was an old-timer, Pap thought that with a new engine and some repairs it might be put into fair shape, and so he made a deal with Dave.

The next day we ran Dave up to Ell Cove on Baranof Island, where he had a shack on the beach. We helped him move his things into the cabin and, bidding him good-by, we headed for home. A few days afterward Dave rowed down to Warm Springs Bay in his skiff and went on a "toot." A week later, after standing drinks for the little settlement, he was broke. He rowed back up to his shack in Ell Cove with a hangover, a big box of magazines, and a new radio battery to help pass time during the isolation of the coming winter. But he had no regrets; he had broken the monotony for a little while and now he was going back to the kind of life he preferred to live.

The *Vanguard* was powered with a big single-cylinder Fairbanks-Morse. Those big brutes were called "stamp-mills" or "rock-crushers" and this one developed around twelve horsepower. There seems to be no wear-out to this type of engine, for they can be kept going with simple improvisations of string and wire. There was nothing mechanically wrong with the engine and it would, in all probability, last another forty years; but the *whooosh* and jar of it firing shook the whole boat, threatened the rigging, and caused one to worry about the caulking coming out of the seams. At any rate, Pap decided to replace it with a high-speed engine and ordered a six-cylinder Chrysler marine engine from town. When it arrived we boys quit fishing and helped Pap remove the old "stamp-mill" and install the new Chrysler. Exchanging engines was not an easy task for us, for we had never done this type of work before. We had only a vague idea of how to go about it, so we decided we'd better talk to Paul. "The most important thing," Paul said, "is getting the new engine properly lined up on the bed-logs. If you don't, you ruin the bearings and oil seal in the reduction gear. Another thing, you'll have to replace the propeller; the diameter and pitch must be for a specific engine." This was something that had never occurred to us.

That night as Pap and I walked home we were over-whelmed by our ignorance. "Well, we got to learn," Pap said at last.

We decided that while we were at it we might as well replace the old shaft, stuffing-box, and stern-bearing. Paul had also advised us to install a fresh-water cooling system, explaining that the engine would last a lot longer than if it were cooled with sea water. We sent to Juneau for these parts, then had to wait until they came on the mailboat two weeks later.

By this time the season was getting along, and we hurried to get the *Vanguard* finished so that we could go fishing. But the work went slowly. Finally, on September twelfth, we were through, and we took the *Vanguard* out for a trial run. We had to make a few minor adjustments, but all in all we were quite satisfied with the job.

Dutch moved aboard the *Vanguard* with Pap, and Duke and I continued to fish the *Resolute*. But we did not do too well; it was fall now, and our plugs and spoons were not catching fish. Paul told us that we would have to start "choking" herring for the king salmon, and we soon learned that it was an art in itself. Patiently, Paul tried to show us, but nine out of ten of our herring would act erratic in the water and seemed to hold little interest for the elusive salmon.

We continued to fish, even though we were catching only a small percentage of fish that the other fishermen were bringing in daily. It was disheartening to watch the rest of them unload their big catches at night, while we had made barely enough to pay for the fuel we had burned. More and more we began to realize that, although a good deal of luck was involved, you had to have the know-how—and learning this took time.

On the twentieth of September the cannery and cold storage stopped operation, and the crew began putting everything away for the winter. This meant an end to our fishing. The weather had been getting progressively worse, and now with the equinoctial storms, most of the boats were calling it a season and leaving, some to their homes in Sitka and Juneau and Petersburg, others to as far away as Seattle.

We had been in Alaska six months now and, thinking back, I realized that it had been not at all as I had expected. But we had not done too badly, for *cheechakoes,* and we had learned a great deal from our mistakes. That was worth something. Next season shouldn't be quite so hard for us. We had proved that we were tough enough to take this hazardous fishing life. Now we must see if we could also live off the land; for as soon as the big Fairbanks-Morse generator at the cannery was shut down and the company store closed, we'd be on our own. Our staples would come from Juneau on the mailboat *Yakobi* which made the trip once a week, weather permitting. But Paul Stromgren advised us not to count upon this too much, for when the winter storms came, weeks sometimes might go by without a boat.

Venison would be our mainstay and the rest of the meal must be built around it. The deer season had already opened, and we boys were anxious to sight in our rifles and go after them. The brown bear were out too; Ma had reported as many as six at a time fishing for salmon in the creek near the house. She carried a .30/06 rifle with her now whenever she went to the creek for water. The rifle might have bolstered Ma's courage, but she knew nothing of firearms and would have been better off without it. This was something we would remedy, for she would be alone a great deal in this country and must learn to shoot reasonably well.

Ducks and geese were flying south on their way down from the interior, and Paul said that a great many wintered in Surprise Harbor and Murder Cove. For the first time since coming north we had time to stand on our legs and look at the country about us. The word *Alaska* is derived from an old Aleut word, meaning "great land," and even this small insignificant strip of coastline hugging Canada had all the earmarks of being just that.

5
THE BROWN BEAR

Admiralty Island is in the Alexander Archipelago of southeastern Alaska, and its sixteen-hundred square miles is home to four species of grizzly bear, as well as the famed Shiras Brown Bear. Interbreeding has produced any number of color variations from light-brown to almost-black. Since these animals depend almost wholly upon spawning salmon of summer and fall to lay on fat for winter hibernation, they are confined pretty much to the larger streams, the nearby beaches, and the peninsulas. When there are no salmon they feed upon skunk cabbage and berries, as well as winter-killed deer carcasses, or perhaps a dead seal or sea lion that has floated in on the tide. These brownies often are rated as the most vicious game animals on earth. One thing is sure: if wounded or cornered, or a female with cub, this bear is about the most dangerous animal I know of. It is also significant that there are *no* black bear found on these same islands inhabited by their larger cousins.

We did not know it on that fine fall morning when Pap and we three boys set out on our first deer hunt, but we were soon to open a deadly war with our brown bear neighbors, a fight that persists sporadically to this day, some fifteen years later. We had not gone more than a hundred yards from the house when Duke looked back over his shoulder and saw a brownie by the creek near our water hole. Although Ma had reported them in force during the early fall, this was the first we had seen since coming home.

"Well," Pap said, "we just as well start cleaning out a few of them from around the house. You saw him first, Duke. Take him!"

The bear was perhaps a hundred and fifty yards away, oblivious to us. We all put cartridges into the chambers of our rifles and started walking slowly toward him. He was big. Real big. There is no animal on the North American continent as awesome as these huge carnivores. When we were within one hundred yards of the animal, a trick of the breeze must have carried our scent to him, and he rose majestically upon hind legs and faced us.

"Holy cow!" Dutch exclaimed in a hushed voice. "It's big as a horse!"

"Now!" Pap said, and Duke knelt and rested an elbow on knee to shoot.

"Where should I shoot him?" Duke whispered, his rifle barrel wavering.

"Now, just take it easy," Pap said calmly. "Brace yourself well, then hold right about where you judge his heart to be."

Barrooom! At the shot the brownie went down into the creek, flopped over, then lunged to its feet and came straight toward us in that lumbering run characteristic of these animals and so deceptively slow. We had spread out so that we would not be in each other's lines of fire; now we began to shoot in earnest, trying to put down the charging brownie that was getting larger by the second in our sights. Even Dutch was banging away with his .25/20. Duke and I were using .30/06s with 180-grain bullets, and they were hurting the bear, but still he came. Suddenly, at perhaps thirty yards, the brownie went down. He struggled to regain his feet, then the massive head slumped and he lay quiet.

We all stood there in silence for a long moment; there was not a one of us that was not deeply shaken by the amount of killing this bear had taken. Dutch had killed the big bear soon after we had come to Surprise Harbor with a single shot from the little .25/20, but it had taken a total of seventeen bullets to get this one down. Blood poured from the many holes in the dark hide. Ma, who had gone to the window at the sound of our rifles, had seen the whole thing and was terrified. She came from the house with Spot, who bristled and tried to grab the huge beast by the throat and shake it. It was the comedy relief we needed, and it broke the silence.

Ma went in to make a pot of coffee, and after a little we followed her inside and sat around talking of the bear until the pot was empty. We boys began arguing as to whose hide it was, and Pap said, "You can fight over the bear hide this evening, but let's get on with the deer hunting. My mouth has been watering all summer for a prime venison steak."

Paul Stromgren had told us that Bartlett Point, on the extreme end of the peninsula that separated Surprise Harbor and Murder Cove, was an excellent place to find deer. But he also told us that it took two men to "drive" it properly. The deer, he said, sometimes came down from the higher ridges early in the morning and late in the evenings, and if any deer had gone onto the point during the night it would be hard for them to get away from us. What Pap proposed, was that two of us would go around the point and then come back through the brush, thus driving whatever deer there might be ahead of us. The other two would wait at a small open sand spit that served to separate the point from the peninsula itself; it was a natural stand, and these two men would have the pick of the deer as they broke across the spit to the protection of the brushy peninsula beyond.

After drawing straws, Duke and Dutch won the privilege of waiting at the spit, and took places behind a five-foot drift log—a log that was to be our favorite stand for years to come. Pap and I split up and began to skirt each side of the point.

On the far end we met and started back through, the slight southeast breeze at our backs driving our scent ahead of us. We were halfway through the heavy brush and timber of the point when Pap, some fifty yards to my left, whistled sharply and pointed ahead to a small knoll. I studied it a long moment before seeing the buck standing quietly behind a tree, head out, watching us. My heart began to pound, and my hands shook. I took a deep breath and threw up my rifle, waited until the wavering front sight settled on the brisket, then squeezed the trigger. The buck bolted, then wheeled suddenly and bounded over the knoll out of sight. I was crestfallen. I silently cursed myself for missing such an easy shot, while Pap came over my way and we walked together on up the knoll.

We found the spot where he'd been standing, and Pap began looking over the area. "Look here," he said at last, "you've hit him!" I trotted over to Pap's side, and there on a fern was a spot of blood. Several feet away was another, then we lost the trail completely. We went up over the knoll, and there in an opening lay my buck, a fine three-pointer. He was dead. There is no describing the elation I felt, and at that moment I would have been hard to touch with a ten-foot pole. It was the first deer I had ever killed.

Pap handed me the makings, and we rolled cigarettes and lit them. "You hit him in the brisket, and he's bled out inside the chest cavity, but you better cut his throat so that you can pull out the windpipe when you dress him," Pap said.

I rolled the buck over onto his back, and taking out my hunting knife, ripped open the abdomen. When I cut through the diaphragm the blood poured out, and a moment later I found that the bullet had pierced the heart.

As I finished dressing the buck we heard Duke's .30/06 boom, then the lighter bark of Dutch's .25/20. Dutch shot ten times, and Pap said, "I wonder what the trouble is—maybe he's flustered and can't hit it."

When we had my buck dressed, Pap took my rifle

and I tried getting the buck on my shoulder, but I had trouble carrying it that way. Finally I grabbed it by the horns and began to drag it. When we got to the spit we heard Duke yell, and a moment later he came running toward us, whooping at the top of his lungs, "I got a big three-pointer!" he yelled. "And Dutch shot at a forked-horn ten times and he got away!"

About that time Dutch came out of the woods on the peninsula side of the spit. He walked slowly toward us, head down, and we knew that he had not found the buck. "I *know* I hit him!" Dutch said. "I know it."

"See any blood?" Pap asked.

Dutch shook his head. "But I know I hit him."

"Well, Wayne can help Duke dress his buck, and I'll go with you and we'll see if we can find the trail."

The two of them went back into the woods, and Duke and I turned back to his deer. We were about to begin dressing it when we heard the sound of an outboard motor. We left the buck and walked over to the water's edge. Paul Stromgren was coming in his skiff. A few minutes later he beached the skiff at our feet and tied the skiff rope to a drift log. "I heard so many shots over this way I thought you boys might have run into a brownie."

We told Paul about killing the big brownie that morning, and then led him over to where our deer lay. He said we both had nice bucks, and sat down to smoke as we began to dress Duke's buck. Our efforts must have been pitiful, for after a moment he said: "You boys mind if I show you how to dress a deer?"

Not at all, we told him. "Well, first thing you want to do is skin off the pads, these scent pads here on the inside of the hind legs. They'll taint the meat. Then rip the skin here between the hind legs and cut through the meat so's you can split the H-bone. Sometimes it's kind of hard to get just the right spot, but when you get her right, it will usually pop right open with the blade of your knife." He felt for the seam in the H-bone with the tip of his knife blade, and when he found it, popped it open in one deft motion. "There, that's the worst part of it." As we watched, Paul worked swiftly, stopping to show us exactly how he did a certain thing, and in a very short time he was finished.

Pap and I had dressed my buck much like we had dressed animals back on the farm, but I could readily see that Paul had a real system here.

"Ever seen a deer-pack?" Paul asked.

"No."

"Easiest way to pack them in this country—especially these small coast deer. They seldom go over a hundred fifty pounds dressed, and if you make them up into a pack you can carry them a good distance." Paul knelt and ripped the skin on the inside of the front legs up to the knee, then skinned out the leg and disjointed it, leaving the hoof and leg bone connected by the strip of skin. He then severed the hind feet at the knee joint, and made a long slit in the skin between the leg bone and the hamstring. "Take the right front foot now, and draw it through this slit in the left hind leg; do the same with the other pair—and you have a ready-made pack sack."

It was simplicity itself. I went to my buck and, with Paul helping, made it up into a pack. When I was through, Paul said, "You can throw the heart and liver into the body cavity now—a fine place to carry and not lose them."

We all walked over to the water's edge to wash the blood from our hands and light a smoke.

"How many deer do you think you've killed, Paul?" Duke asked.

"Oh, I really don't know," Paul said matter-of-factly, "a man living out in the brush like this doesn't hunt much for sport . . . I just go out and shoot one when I run out of meat. I suppose I've killed a couple of hundred or so."

We smoked on, each silent with our own thoughts, and pretty soon Paul said, "Well, guess I'd better get home, I'm corning venison—or supposed to be." He grinned at us and untied his skiff. "You boys watch those brownies real close; they're nothing to fool with. Some of them—like that one this morning—take a lot of killing. Ever kill a hog? Hit it just right the first shot, and a .22 short will do the job . . . but if you hit it wrong, it gets worked up and you'll have the devil's own time putting it down. Bear is the same way. Deer too—any animal, for the matter, or man. Look at Rasputin." He grinned at us again and pushed his skiff out away from the beach with an oar. "If a brownie ever gets you dead-to-rights, don't move! Don't move an eyelid; movement is what sets them off."

He started the outboard motor, waved, and headed back across Murder Cove. Duke and I finished our smokes and walked slowly back across the spit to where the deer lay. "You reckon we'll ever know as much as Paul knows?" he asked.

I looked out across Chatham Strait to the jutting outline of Baranof Island. It was eight miles away but it looked like you could reach out and touch it. The sun touched a thousand facets and each snowy ridge stood bold and clear; up high the wind was lifting snow from the peaks in plumes. I knew then that I loved this country, and though I might get tired of it and go away at times, I'd always come back. This was home.

"You think we ever will?" Duke asked.

"What?" I said.

"Know half as much as Paul."

"I reckon we will, in time," I said, and we helped each other into the deer-packs that Paul had shown us how to make, and, rifles in hand, we went down the beach toward home.

We were sitting at the table having a cup of coffee

when we saw Pap and Dutch coming home. Dutch was staggering under the weight of a good-sized forked-horn that he carried awkwardly over one shoulder. He dumped the buck alongside ours in the woodshed and then followed Pap inside the house.

"I got him!" Dutch said triumphantly.

"Yeah," Pap said, reaching for the coffee pot, "he must have dropped from the sheer weight of the lead he was packing. Dutch hit him seven times when he first shot, then when we ran onto him again on the peninsula, he hit him five more. That .25/20 is worthless. I still can't understand how he ever killed that big brownie with it this spring." He turned to Dutch. "I think you best throw it out into the bay before you run into a mean bear and get killed."

After we finished lunch Duke and I took Dutch outside and showed him how to make his buck up into a pack. Dutch sat down on the steps of the woodshed, leaned backward, and put his arms through the natural straps that the deer's crossed legs made. He stood up with the buck riding high on his shoulders, and turned to grin at us. "Pretty slick, isn't it! Look, I've got both of my arms free!"

I had been thinking the same thing. If I was out in the brush with a deer on my back, I sure wanted to be ready to shoot straight and fast if a brownie suddenly rose up in front of me.

That evening the three of us sharpened our hunting

knives and began skinning out the brownie. It was a real job, and it was almost supper time before we finished. Then, with Pap's help, we rigged a block-and-tackle and began inching the bear carcass back into the brush. It was dark before this was done, and we dug a shallow pit and rolled the carcass in and covered it. The hide squared nine feet, and we decided to flesh and smoke it a little to cure it before putting it down on the living-room floor.

Late that night I awoke to hear old Spot whining and scratching at the door. I lay in my bunk listening. Then I heard it, a roaring every now and then from the direction of the creek. I reached over and shook Duke.

"What's up?" he asked.

"I don't know," I said, "but I'm going to find out. Get up and get dressed."

When we had our clothes on, we took our rifles from the rack on the wall and stepped outside. I had the five-cell flashlight, and Duke and I began to walk toward the creek. Spot was a few feet ahead, the hair on his back sticking straight up, and he was growling deep down in his chest. About halfway we stopped a moment to listen and heard snarling and a crunching of bones. We went on cautiously, then a moment later the beam of the flashlight found the source of the disturbance. Across the creek some thirty yards away were four brownies snapping and snarling at one another as they ate the dead bear. They glared balefully at the light, but otherwise paid little attention. We watched them for several minutes, until one of them became annoyed with the light and advanced slowly toward us. Duke and I backed carefully away, rifles ready to shoot if we had to. Presently the brownie turned and ran back to the others. It lunged at one of its companions, who might have eaten more than his share. They reminded me of a bunch of dogs fighting over a bone.

They were gone at daylight, but the next night they were back once more to finish their gruesome feast. We were later to learn that there was nothing peculiar about this, for brownies are notorious cannibals. They are not gregarious by nature, and seem to relish nothing quite so much as eating one of their own.

On the fourth night they were joined by two more brownies, and all the quarreling and fighting that ensued kept us awake and did not endear us to our cannibalistic neighbors. We did not dare shoot another, however, for we knew that would start the whole thing all over again. And you do not just grab a seven- or eight-hundred-pound bear by the leg and drag it away.

When every last bit of flesh and bone had been devoured, the marauders paused to lick their chops and then turned their noses in the direction of our woodshed, from which the scent of venison must have been enticing indeed.

6
BEAR,
AND MORE BEAR

Several nights went by without incident, then late one
night Duke woke me, and said: "There's something
fooling around in the woodshed." I climbed out of my
sleeping bag and pulled on a wool shirt. Old Spot was

whining softly at the door. The woodshed was actually a lean-to, open at the end, built against the side of the house. I pushed Spot away and eased the door open a crack. In the dim moonlight I saw the indistinct shapes of two bears eating our deer. My heart quickened and began to pound. Their unpleasant, musky odor filled my nostrils, and I shivered uncontrollably. I quietly closed the door and turned to Duke.

"Bears," I whispered. "Get your oh-six ready. I'll ease the door open and hold the light on them for you."

When he was ready I slowly opened the door once more—and flicked on the light. Both bears looked up from their eating straight into the light. I was in front of Duke and I jumped aside and yelled: "Shoot!"

Spot broke between Duke's legs just as he pulled the trigger, and the shot went through the woodshed roof. The bears exploded into action, coming within a few feet of us as they ran out of the shed and across the garden to disappear into the brush.

It had happened so quickly, Duke did not have time for another shot. Spot followed as far as the garden and stopped to bark for a couple of hours, thus showing the intruders that they had scared him not at all. Ma was calling from inside the house, and lighting a lamp. Pap and Dutch were wanting to know what the shooting was about.

The deer had been badly chewed, a fact that made us wonder how we could possibly have slept while the carnivores munched and cracked bones only a few feet away. The next three nights we boys took turns standing watch, but the bears did not appear. On the fourth night, after we had said, "We must have scared the devil out of them—they won't be back," they came and, this time, with a friend.

Dutch heard them, and woke Duke and me. We pulled on our boots first, for the last time I had run outside barefooted and stepped on a nail. Pap heard us and asked, "What's up, boys?" "Bear!" I said, and pushed the growling Spot into one of the back bedrooms and closed the door. Then Duke and I took rifles from the rack on the wall and stepped quietly to the back door. We had rehearsed just what we would do if the marauders came back, so each man knew his job and there was no confusion. Dutch had the five-cell flashlight, but he did not turn it on until we eased the back door open. Duke and I stepped quietly out into the back yard and waited several paces apart. When Dutch's flashlight went on, three brownies were so busy working on the one mangled deer carcass we'd left for bait, they hardly looked up. Duke and I put our sights upon the two front ones and shot. One went down immediately, but the other two lunged off the porch and started across the garden, one carrying the deer carcass in his mouth much like a dog might carry a rabbit. Dutch ran out of the doorway and kept the beam of his light upon them. One was obviously wounded. Duke and I got them in our sights and began shooting again. The wounded one went down in Ma's cabbage patch and the one with the deer dropped it and ran into the woods roaring and bellowing at the top of his lungs. Duke and I both claimed to have hit him.

As we stood there a moment getting our breath, Dutch turned with the light and saw the brownie on the porch trying to get to its feet. He screamed for us to shoot, and we wheeled together and each put a shot into the massive head. Ma and Pap were lighting lamps and calling to us, and Dutch went back to explain what had happened. Duke and I walked out to the garden to where the other bear lay. I put the muzzle of my rifle against the big head and fired. We were learning.

Out in the woods the wounded brownie continued to roar. From the sound we could tell he was slowly circling the house.

"I wouldn't go back there after him now, for all the money in the world," Duke said, shivering.

"Me either," and I thought of all the terrifying tales I'd heard and read about wounded brown bears.

We went back to the porch where the others stood looking at the brownie that lay there flooding the floor with its blood. The wounded bear kept roaring with rage out in the woods and I felt a shiver go down my spine. Tomorrow we'd have to take old Spot, trail the bear and kill him, but I sure didn't relish the chore of going into the brush after him.

The next day, after we had dragged the brownie from the porch and skinned it, we took our rifles and, with Spot in the lead, set out on the wounded bear's trail. It had circled the house at a distance of perhaps seventy-five yards, then veered and crossed the creek. We took it slow and easy, our eyes on Spot who had an extraordinary nose for a terrier. The trail turned and twisted with no set direction; sometimes we found blood, sometimes not. At last we came to a thicket of blueberry brush, devil club, and small stunted cedar.

"I'll lay odds," Pap said, "that he's holed up in there."

Spot, nose still to the trail, limped into the thicket and was soon lost from sight. A minute later we heard him barking; it was not his excited yip-yip bark.

"What do you boys think?" Pap asked.

We all agreed that he had found the bear, and that it evidently represented no danger.

"Well, let's spread out a little," Pap said, "and take it slow and easy."

Sixty yards inside the thicket we found Spot sitting on his haunches looking at the dead bear, already starting to stiffen. We all breathed a big sigh of relief.

When we got home we began skinning out the bear we had killed in the garden; both brownies had long, dark-brown hair, and we decided to smoke-tan their hides and put them on the front-room floor. The one we had already would go on our bedroom floor. But now we were back facing our old problem: what to do with the carcasses. Both bears weighed in excess of seven hundred pounds, we guessed, the larger one possibly eight hundred pounds. To haul them out into the woods would be inviting their cronies to another feast—and that, we decided, we could do without. At last Pap suggested that we bury a "deadman" on the beach in front of the house for a tail-hold, then with block-and-tackle we could drag the carcasses out to where the high tide would float them. Then it would be no job to tow them out into the bay with the skiff and outboard motor. We did this and, when we were through with the chore, Duke spoke for all of us when he said: "I've had about all I want of bears for a while."

Late September is a time of change; summer has gone, and winter is not too far ahead. It is a time of equinoctial storms and sudden rain squalls. By October the morning air is crisp and, up high, the ridges show frost. The deer begin to move downward just ahead of the frost line, and this is the best time of the year for the hunter.

During the late summer we had brought in silver salmon, called *cohos*, and Ma had canned several cases of them. We had invested in a home-canning machine and twenty-five cases of cans; we intended to fill the rest of the cans with venison, ducks, geese, and with clams from the nearby clam bed on the spit at Deer Island. We also had some special enameled cans for crab meat, and we built several crab pots and set

them out in the bay. Although in many ways we were
green to this country, we had come from a farm and
knew how to put up winter food. Venison would take
the place of beef and pork, and the big, fat Sitka Black-
tail bucks were plentiful. We boys were doing all of the
game hunting and packing—and we loved every minute
of it. Ma and Pap began putting it up for winter use.

Venison chops and roasts were canned and processed, the scraps ground and made into hamburger
and chili, which were also canned. Pap had several big
crocks and one of these held salted king salmon sides
that we'd put down in the early fall to be soaked out
and smoked or baked at a later date. The other crocks
were for corned venison and sugar-cured venison hams.
It is surprising how much like pork venison tastes when
it is smoked and later fried or baked. We ordered side
pork out from town on the mailboat, then ground and
mixed it equally with venison. This made a delicious
sausage, which we seasoned and either packed for
smoking into small cheesecloth bags that Ma made, or
else made it into patties and partly fried it before packing them into a large crock and covering the patties
completely with lard. Either method kept the meat well
and it could be used as needed.

Paul Stromgren had shown us how to make a deer-
call, and we began using it with great success. A call
will bring a doe within range, nine times out of ten.
It will also bring a buck as rutting season nears, but he

is much more cautious and will rarely show himself if there is any cover. It will even bring a brownie who, with a shortage of salmon in the streams, has developed a taste for venison. Duke found this out one day as he was sitting upon the edge of a muskeg blowing his deer-call.

The day before on this same muskeg, he had called up a particularly fine buck and killed it. Now he was back, trying for another. He had blown the call off and on for some minutes but nothing had shown. He put out his cigarette and was ready to leave when a strange musky odor came to his nostrils. As he sat there trying to identify it, he became aware of something at his back, and at precisely the same moment he recalled the odor of the brownies we'd killed. Something touched his back, and then he could hear the bear sniffing the dried deer blood of yesterday's buck. He wished suddenly that he'd changed his wool hunting shirt. His reaction was to jump up and run, but he knew better than that. He glanced at his .30/06 leaning against a rotten stump three feet away—it might just as well have been a mile. Then, as his self-control was about to break, he recalled Paul's words: *If a brownie ever gets you dead-to-rights, don't move! Don't move an eyelid; movement is what sets them off.*

For several long minutes he sat there with the hot breath of the bear on his neck as it continued to sniff him. His reprieve finally came when a fawn called from

across the far side of the muskeg. The bear moved away
a few yards, and ever so slowly Duke turned his head
and saw the animal for the first time. It was big—larger
perhaps than any of the ones we had killed. When the
brownie had moved off fifty yards, Duke eased to his
left and got his rifle. He slipped a cartridge into the
chamber with trembling fingers and sat there quietly
watching the bear until it was out of sight.

A week later we had a still closer call. We had by
now slashed out a fair trail across the peninsula to
Murder Cove. On this particular morning I had elected
to stay home, and the rest of the family set out on the
weekly trip to the cannery to collect the mail. They
moved along the trail single file, Duke in the lead
with the only rifle, then Ma, Pap, and Dutch.

They were midway along the trail when, without
warning or apparent provocation, a huge brownie rose
up from behind a log where it had been lying and
charged straight for them. When Duke first saw the
animal, it was perhaps thirty-five feet away, and by the
time his rifle came to shoulder it was almost upon them.
He flipped off the safety, and shot. The bullet hit the
animal squarely in the chest, staggered it, but still it
came. He shot twice more into the chest, but each time
it recovered from the smashing impact of the 220-grain
bullet and came on resolutely. Finally he shot it in the
head and for the first time it went down. But the next
moment it was up again. Duke put another shot again

into the massive head and was now hardly a barrel's length away. As the brownie slid forward to the ground it knocked Duke backward and he too went down.

He twisted on the ground and threw the remaining cartridge into the chamber, but it was not needed; it was all over. The whole thing had taken less than a minute during which the rest of the family had scarcely moved.

I have been told by some that a female brownie does not attain any real size; this female's hide, however, squared eleven feet, and we estimated she weighed somewhere near twelve hundred pounds. It was the largest brownie I have seen in this part of the country, and by far the largest bear any of us were to kill in several years of hunting these carnivores. And it brought to our attention another facet of the strange, unpredictable behavior of these animals. The bear had been waiting behind the large log, watching the trail. Had it been waiting for a deer to pounce upon, or had it become separated from a cub and turned its frustrations upon the first moving thing it saw? But there was one thing we did know: the head shots had put the bear down!

When first we had decided to come to Alaska, we boys had read every article we could find on brown bears. I still remember one of the things almost always preached: *Never* shoot a brown bear in the head, for its brain is located at the base of the sloping skull and so protected by thick bone that the bullet will glance off.

This is pure fiction. I do not know what started the story that a bullet would glance off a bear's skull. Perhaps the perpetrator made a bad shot; again, it might have resulted from the use of one of the old slow-moving calibers. At any rate, it is certainly untrue of today's high-speed rifles—except perhaps in rare instances. It is true that a bear's skull is long and sloping, and that its brain is well protected from a frontal shot. But this certainly does not mean that it is invulnerable; a modern rifle will shatter the bones of the head to such a degree that the nerve centers are bound to be seriously affected. An enraged brownie with its heart shot out is still a dangerous animal. It may travel a hundred yards before bleeding to death, and an animal that has time to do this is easily capable of killing its foe before dying itself. But a head shot, as a rule, will put a bear down, if it does not kill it outright, thus giving the shooter time for another shot. An ear shot such as Dutch had made accidentally with his little .25/20 illustrated how easily a bear may be killed if hit squarely in the ear. The record shows that a surprising number of brownies have been killed by a shot in the ear from a .22 rifle.

Shortly after this encounter we made a rule that has served us well: *if the bear is inside the safety margin, and appears dangerous—shoot it in the head.* And we all carried a .30/06 rifle when we thought we might run into a brownie. It is my opinion that a man is foolish if he hunts with a rifle any smaller. All of us have killed brown bears with everything from a .22 Hornet on up, but it was only because it was all we had to shoot with at the time. With a smaller caliber rifle one must stand fast and place his shots. But sometimes a man does not have the time, and he must shoot by instinct alone.

The first occasion on which I had a chance to test my speed with a rifle—and my courage as well—was very nearly my last. It happened shortly after Duke's encounter with the big she-bear on the trail. I was deer hunting and was packing in a nice buck I had taken. I was still unfamiliar with the ridges behind Surprise Harbor, and in the vastness of the woods I got turned around. I knew, however, that all the streams in the country led eventually to the beach, and I decided to follow out the first creek I came to.

Before I came to a creek I ran into several acres of windfalls, the result of an exceptionally bad storm some years before. In my ignorance I thought I might cross the downed timber without too much difficulty, but soon I found it would be practically impossible to cross the obstacle course with the deer upon my back. I had turned about and was starting back, when suddenly I heard brush cracking on the far side of a log pile. It never entered my mind that it might be anything but a deer; and, likewise, I did not consider how I would find my way back to the spot if it was a deer and I killed it. I slipped off the safety on my rifle, and stepped quietly around the end of the log pile.

There, facing me, not fifteen feet away, was a brownie. We stared at each other for a long moment. I did not want to shoot at such short range if it was at all possible to avoid it. But the bear apparently wasn't going to be the first to turn away; the scent of the freshly killed buck upon my back must have been enticing. The hair of the brownie's hump began to rise, and my finger tightened on the trigger. At its first lunge I shot at the massive head. The next moment I was knocked sideways and the crushing weight of the deer came down on top of me. I lifted my head slowly and looked around. The brownie was several yards away, watching me malevolently and coughing blood. My right hand still gripped my rifle, but with the weight of the deer upon my back I dared not try to reload and move into a position to fire. I lay still, scarcely breathing, and wondered how hard I had hit the bear. From what I could see I'd missed the head and hit the throat. My thoughts went to old man Hasselburg at Mole Harbor who had been so badly mauled by a brownie.

The coughing continued for several long moments, then finally the huge head began to drop. I waited until the animal had fallen to the ground, then slipped slowly out of the deer-pack. I did not really begin to breathe freely until I had put another bullet into the big head. I was bruised but not so much as scratched.

And it was not just Duke, Dutch, and I that seemed to draw brownies; eventually both Ma and Pap had their troubles with them. Pap, while goose hunting in the high grass flats of Murder Cove, almost stepped on a dozing bear that rose up and came straight for him. He quickly dispatched it with a number-two shot; a 12-gauge shotgun is a formidable weapon at short range. The following summer Ma was to kill a big brownie that had dominated the creek while the rest of us were away fishing. After two days without water she rigged herself a shooting bench on the back porch. She waited patiently until Mister Brownie ambled out into sight, then clobbered him with an extraordinary shot in the head.

After killing so many bears in the vicinity of Surprise Harbor, we began to breathe more freely, although we never went into the woods unarmed. We were to have encounters with them from time to time throughout the years to come, but never again would they trouble us the extent they did that first fall.

7
WINTER

In August, Ma had sent away for accredited Home
Study Courses for Duke and Dutch. When they finally
arrived in October, she was hard put getting school
started. Both of the boys were imaginative enough to

have plenty of excuses to postpone the starting date: they must bring in more deer to put up, for it would be a long winter and we didn't want to run out; Pap needed help doing this or that, and so on and on. Dutch even *volunteered* to cut more firewood, although the woodshed was full and we had several cords stacked nearby.

It is doubtful if Ma would ever have got them started had she not used a little psychology. The three of us had all ordered custom-made seal-hunting rifles from a big gunshop in Seattle, and they had just arrived. They were bull-barreled .220 Swifts with ten-power scopes. We also had ordered reloading equipment; press, dies, scales, fifty pounds of various rifle powders, hundreds of bullets and primers. The three of us were enthusiastically planning to take the *Resolute* and go over to Tracy and Endicott Arms on the mainland, and bounty-hunt for seals in the spring. We had not forgotten how much money Fred Manly and Cliff Kilkenny had made seal hunting.

It was an adventure that we all were looking forward to, and Ma took full advantage of this. One day she informed Duke and Dutch that school was starting at eight o'clock the following morning. When they both began to protest, she simply said that if they wanted to go seal hunting in April, they had better get busy with their studies. I helped Ma out by saying since it was already October, they couldn't possibly finish their school year by the first of April. And that it sure was going to be fun hunting all those seal by myself. This made them stop and think, and at last they decided that they must do a lesson and a half a day in order to get finished by April. And so Ma's school began.

The garden had done very well. In the spring we had taken Paul Stromgren's advice and buried kelp and starfish and herring in our garden spot; this had made excellent fertilizer. The long summer days and the sun had done the rest. We had lettuce and radishes and onions, fine potatoes and carrots and turnips, as well as rutabagas and cabbage. With the first frost we built a root cellar and began to store the root vegetables and cabbage. To keep them from freezing we built bins on the floor of the cellar and packed them among dry grass, then covered the bins with more grass and earth.

The cans we had bought were full of venison and fish and crab meat. We had Mason jars of minced clams from the clam bed near Deer Island, and there were several cases of blueberry jelly, sugared salmonberries, and wild crab apple jelly. Our crocks were filled with salted king salmon, pickled herring, corned venison, and preserved sausage. We had only to order staples out from town—things like flour and sugar and coffee. All in all we were well provisioned for the coming winter.

Late fall. The feel of winter is heavy in the air. The brown bear have gone to their hibernation beds and we won't be troubled with them again until spring once more is upon us. The snow on the higher slopes has driven the deer down to lower ground and they are beginning to appear regularly on the beaches, sometimes nibbling on kelp at low tide. We see does and last spring's fawns, yearlings, big bucks that are beginning to drop their antlers. As if sensing that they are safe, they show little fear of us and usually stand their ground and curiously give us the eye. These bucks are different animals now, docile almost, with none of the fire of such a short time ago. Perhaps the loss of antlers has a psychological effect upon them.

Land-otter tracks are to be seen in the first light snows, and we find their slides on the hillsides where they play. We see their dens and feeding spots, and on occasion we even see them snatch a feeding duck or seagull from a flock beneath the water. There is a frenzied squawk and flapping of wings, then the bird disappears and presently one spots the otter heading for its den with dinner in its mouth. Mink are plentiful too, and we see their faint trails along the beach above the high-tide mark. We find where they have eaten sea urchin and small fish and crabs. Pap, who had done a lot of fox and coyote trapping, says that we will do well with trail sets in this country. The trapping season is closed this year, however, and so we must be content to wait until next season.

By degrees the winter slips upon us. This is a land of

snow and ice and bitter-cold northerly winds. But we
have learned now why the old-timers wear nothing but
wool in this country. During the spring and early-fall
rainy season, there is sometimes a rain mist, not heavy
enough to warrant rain gear, and the heavy wool shirt
and trousers seem to soak up the moisture without getting one wet. Wet wool is not too uncomfortable anyway, if one is active. While duck and goose hunting we
boys have often broken through soft ice and been completely soaked. With a bitter wind blowing and temperature below freezing, a person would seem to be a
likely candidate for pneumonia; but this is not so if a
little sense is used. We learned to strip off completely
and wring out all the wet clothing, put it back on, and
then set out for home at a brisk trot. The worst part,
of course, is the stripping-down in a freezing wind, but
once dressed again and on your way, it is only minutes
until your body warms the damp wool and you are not
too uncomfortable. I don't recall any of us ever getting
a cold from such a dunking. The only time we ever got
a cold, or the flu, was on those rare occasions when we
came into contact with someone from town.

Paul had said that this was an unusually bad winter,
and we were ready to believe it. In January there was
first a bad southeast storm that blew for a solid week;
then, overnight, the wind switched to the north and
whistled down from the glacier country for another ten
days. During the summer months we had learned that

a north wind seldom became severe, but now in the middle of the winter it could be savage indeed. During this northerly storm in January we got a preview of just how bad one could become. The *Vanguard* and *Resolute* were anchored in Surprise Harbor in the lee of Deer Island, but this gave them protection only from the southeasterly storms. The bottom was not the best holding ground and the anchors always dragged in a bad blow. Then Pap and I would row out and stand anchor watches, sometimes for two and three days at a stretch. At last we decided to build a cradle and pull the *Resolute* up onto the beach at high water. The *Vanguard*, however, would be kept in reserve in case someone was badly hurt or became sick, and we had to make an emergency run to town.

One day late in January a sudden gust of wind sprang up in the bay as we were having lunch. Half an hour later, when Pap and I had launched the skiff and began rowing for the *Vanguard*, a regular *williwaw* hit. We estimated that gusts were seventy to eighty miles an hour. One gust overturned the skiff and suddenly Pap and I were in the water trying desperately to get our boots off. We managed to swim to the overturned skiff and hang on until the wind blew us ashore a couple of hundred yards from the house. Duke and Dutch and Ma were waiting to help us out, and we hurried to the house and changed into dry clothes. But our troubles were just beginning. Duke called out that the *Van-*

guard was drifting toward the rocky shore of the peninsula.

To lose the *Vanguard* now would be disastrous, for Pap had put his entire savings into it. After what had already happened it would be foolish to try again to get to the boat in the skiff, and the four of us took off running along the wind-swept beach where we thought the *Vanguard* would go aground. Three hundred yards from the house we had to wade the knee-deep water of a sand spit in order to cross onto the peninsula. The *Vanguard* was already aground, rolling heavily as the strong gusts hit her. *We've lost her,* I thought. *She'll break up and sink before we ever get there!*

When we gained the peninsula we ran again, hearts pumping, throats dry, hardly feeling the bitter wind through our wet clothing. When we came to the *Vanguard,* Pap yelled, "All right, into the water, boys! Dutch on the bilge pump while I try to get the engine started. Wayne and Duke, get your shoulders under the guard rail and try to ease her a little!"

We all half waded and half swam out to the boat, and Pap and Dutch pulled themselves aboard. Duke and I stood in the icy water with our shoulders under the guard rail trying to ease her as the swell and the wind relentlessly tried to push her higher upon the rocky beach. We could feel her shudder and creak every time she came down with a jar upon the rocks.

Pap came on deck after a few minutes. "The battery

was under water and the wiring and the distributor are damp," he yelled above the wind. "I've moved the battery—don't think much salt water got into it, but I'll never get the engine started unless I can somehow dry the wiring and distributor out a little. How long can you boys hold out there?"

Duke and I looked at each other. "Go ahead and see what you can do, Pap," I said. "We'll stay as long as we can."

A half-hour later we hear Pap grinding away with the starter. It didn't sound very strong. I said a prayer beneath my breath that it would start, and, looking at Duke in the water beside me, I saw his fingers were crossed. A backfire, a puff of black smoke quickly swept away by the wind, then it caught suddenly, and we knew Pap was tending the choke and throttle with all the skill in him. It was only hitting on five cylinders now, but it was running.

When the engine had smoothed down a little Pap stepped out upon the back deck. "All right," he said, "I don't know how badly she's damaged on the bottom, and she might sink if we are able to get her off the rocks, but we'll lose her for sure if we don't move her— she'll pound plumb to pieces. When I yell, you boys get aboard and open the hatch and start bailing with buckets. Dutch, you keep busy on that bilge pump. If I can get her off I'll head right for that sandy beach to the left of the house."

A moment later we heard Pap cutting the anchor chain loose. Then he was back in the wheelhouse and we could feel the *Vanguard* shudder as he engaged the clutch and opened the throttle. "Push!" I yelled to Duke, and we both put all of our strength into it. It seemed as if she would never free herself, then a big swell raised her clear and she lurched forward. Duke and I clung to the stern until Dutch helped us aboard.

"The wheel's been damaged on the rocks," Pap yelled, "and I don't dare run the engine too fast, but thank God we didn't lose the rudder!"

Duke and I took off the hatch cover and went into the fish hold with our bailing buckets. Dutch continued pumping on the deck pump. We were just barely making headway against the wind, and little by little Pap inched the *Vanguard* toward the sandy beach near the house. When at last the bow stem hit, I jumped overboard into the shallow water with a long line and made it fast to a tree.

But our ordeal was not yet over, for the tide was still flooding and we still had to continue to pump and bail and keep the water from getting farther up on the engine. Pap stayed on the bow to keep pulling the boat higher up on the beach as the flooding tide continued to raise her.

Finally Pap said, "Tide's starting to ebb now, boys, head for the house. I'll be along as soon as I get another line ashore."

We climbed down then, and began wading ashore, the three of us, exhausted, half-frozen, numb. Ma was there to help us up the beach to the wonderful warmth of the house with its dry clothing. It had been a close one, but we had saved the *Vanguard.*

Isolation. We live in a little world all our own. A snowy world, sometimes dazzling in the sunlight, sometimes obscured by a sudden snow flurry. The days are short: it does not get light until nearly nine-thirty in the morning, and by three-thirty in the afternoon we are beginning to use the gas lanterns and kerosene lamps. Pap and I searched the beaches for lumber that has drifted in, and have built a workshop. We spend the short days making furniture for the house—chairs and table, cupboards for Ma, closets. We even engineer a crude wood lathe operated by one of us turning a large crank while another does the cutting. We decided we could turn out wooden fishing plugs as good as the ones for which we paid a dollar twenty-five the past summer, and we turn dozens of them by hand, sand and paint them, then fit them with swivels and hooks.

Isolation is not nearly as boring as one might think. There is no time clock to punch, and in fact we scarcely look at a clock; our day is governed by the daylight hours. Nothing is really pressing, yet we seem always to be busy. Pap and I spend the short days working in the shop or chopping wood. It is amazing how much wood a cook stove and heater can burn when the temperature is low! Duke and Dutch are busy with their schooling, working desperately now to get finished in time to go seal hunting in April. Pap and I have the boats to care for, and there seem always to be new projects coming to mind.

We read omnivorously, and this perhaps is the most important single pursuit during a long winter of isolation. We have subscribed to numerous magazines, as well as book clubs, and we have books sent out from the library in Juneau. Every mailboat has literature of some kind.

One day a large box of books and magazines comes, on the mailboat, from someone along the five-hundred-mile mailboat route who has heard of us settling in Surprise Harbor. We are touched by this thoughtful act, and go through the box with great delight. In return we gather all of the magazines and books that we have finished, and send them off to our new-found friends. Pretty soon we are exchanging literature with people all around the route.

And we have other diversions. Duke and I are learning to play the guitar, Dutch the mandolin. We even talked Ma into learning the harmonica, so we can play together.

What we enjoy most, though, is hurrahing Ma. She is by no means ignorant, but I believe she is the most naïve person I have ever known, and possibly the most gullible, at least as far as we boys are concerned. We have learned that, if we can control our enthusiasm and keep a straight face, she will believe the most outlandish yarns we can possibly think up. We come in from our wanderings with stories of flying mink, of frogs we have seen wearing snowshoes, of snow-white rattlesnakes; we talk until she is firmly hooked, then hurrah her for believing such fiction. But Ma simply says, "Oh, pooh!"

And gambling. There is nothing so enjoyable, perhaps, as gambling for high stakes, and this is one of our favorite pastimes. We play cards to see who does all of the numerous chores, and Ma has learned to put in her bid for water early on washday, for the loser invariably yells, "Misdeal," and it might take another hour or more of serious card playing before this grumbling individual starts for the creek with his neck yoke and two big water pails. There is wood to be carried in and stacked in the wood boxes, kindling to be split for starting fires, gas lanterns and kerosene lamps to be filled for the night.

And on those occasions when we are low on certain staples, we boys divide up our share and play cards for them. Duke, who is most often the loser, will sit and watch Dutch and me casually drop three lumps of sugar into our coffee while he has none, or observe us spread butter thickly upon our toast while he eats his dry. Ma abhors this game, of course, and despite our violent objection, wants to share with the loser.

Sometimes, when boredom is heavy upon us, and when our world appears so utterly remote it is hard to believe there are actually other people upon this planet, we play a game Ma dislikes even more. The loser must go outside and strip to the skin, then climb to the roof of the shed and flap his arms like wings and crow like a rooster before jumping into a deep snow bank. We call this "The Bird Bit," and the other two of us usually snowball the shivering bird and run him off into the woods. This invariably brings Ma raging outside after the epic flight from the roof, swinging her broom at the snowballers and muttering all the while what *damn fools* she had given birth to, and if said naked jaybird dies of pneumonia it will serve him right!

When we are not in the mood for such games there are always the beaches, miles of them, rocky beaches and sandy ones, all like opening a surprise package. Our beaches are open to southeasterly storms, and it is after these storms that they are the most productive. At such times we find various items: skiffs that have drifted in, assorted oars, lumber washed from lumber barges, parts of seines, fishing plugs, halibut flags and buoys, or perhaps a drum of gasoline or diesel oil. I once found a pair of bedroom slippers, Christmas wrapped, and labeled "Mier and Frank, Portland, Oregon."

One day we even found the legendary bottle-with-a-note. We were thinking that this bottle might have come perhaps from a Portuguese fisherman or isolated South Seas beachcomber. But when at last we worked the cork from its mouth and extracted the note, we were disappointed to find it had originated only thirty miles away in Frederick Sound, written by an old Norwegian we had made friends with during the past summer's fishing season.

After much thought, Duke came up with the suggestion of how we might make a good joke of our find. Wheels turned and we sent the note and our instructions to a long-lost relative who lived in Burlington, Iowa, on the Mississippi River. In due course our old Norwegian friend received a letter from a complete stranger who informed him that his bottle-with-note was found floating in a catfish hole of a slough near the banks of the mighty Mississippi.

It was our intention, of course, to wait until the following summer when we would again see our old friend, and by subtle inquiries, learn if he had been hooked by this little joke. If he had, it would be well worth the effort.

When summer came at last, we had all but forgotten the incident. To our surprise the lonely oldster, whose name was Olaf, had been so excited by the letter that he had ordered charts from the States showing the intricate currents of the entire seven seas. The detailed

letter from our Mississippi River relative was framed
and hung over the fireplace, written proof of this won-
drous thing. I quickly pointed out that, between the
time he had written the note until it was found floating
on the Mississippi River, only five months had elapsed.
Duke went on to doubt that one of the fastest sailing
ships of a bygone era could have made it around the
Horn and up the Mississippi in that kind of time. And
then I asked the big question: how could the bottle
have made its way *up* the Mississippi? But nothing we
said could dim Olaf's enthusiasm. He went into a three-
hour discourse of the enigmatic ocean currents, and of
how the bottle probably drifted through the Panama
Canal locks in the wake of a steamer, and so on and
on, all the while tracing its presumed course on nautical
charts.

Our little deception was now clearly beyond the
joking stage but, in one last attempt to stop it before
it got out of hand, I casually asked Olaf if he thought
it possible that someone around our part of the country
could have found his bottle, and might be playing a
joke on him.

"Vat!" Olaf exclaimed, then waved a hand as if I
might be crazy to even think of anything so outlandish.
"Who vould go to soooch trouble—yust for a yoke!"

And so we were committed. We would pick up Olaf's
bottles in the years that followed, sometimes while
searching the beach for a drift after a storm, sometimes

when trapping in the winters. We would hold them until the notes were sufficiently aged, then contact a pen
pal in some far corner of the world, to pass on the
"finds." Our confederates never gave us away, and
whenever we stopped by Olaf's small island, which had
been a fox farm back in the old days, we always took
along a bottle of whisky which Olaf helped us kill. He
would then put in his note, cork it, and have us drop it
over the side on the way home.

Until Olaf passed on to calmer waters at the age of
eighty-six, he periodically sent out his messenger
bottles, although I doubt seriously that any of them ever
got any farther than our beach at Point Gardener.

8
A TRIP TO TOWN

There comes a time in February when every resident of the brush has had more than enough of winter. It does not matter how much he may like his life of independence out in the wilderness, he must confess that

winter is entirely too damned long! Fatigue and frustration and sludging of the blood occur, and, as the snow
banks pile higher and higher, winter repressions likewise pile up almost beyond endurance. At such a time
one must plunge into some new project that will take
him home at night worn out and cold and hungry,
grateful for a warm meal and bed.

Pap and I decided it was time to begin repairing the
Vanguard. We rigged a homemade windlass and pulled
the battered boat above the high-tide mark, then
jacked it to an upright position and shored. Several
ribs had been broken, and on one side some ten planks
had to be replaced. We had ordered fir planking and
bending-oak from Juneau, and, when it came on the
mailboat, we ran the *Resolute* around to the dock at
Tyee and loaded it aboard.

Pap and I were going once again into something we
knew little about. There is all the difference in the
world between a house carpenter and a shipwright, but
as the days went by we learned from our mistakes and
the battered derelict slowly began to show vestiges of
a new life. We had built a steam box on the beach near
the *Vanguard* and connected it to a fifty-gallon oil
drum which, half-filled with water and with a fire beneath, served as a boiler. New oak ribs were laboriously
ripped to size by hand, steamed, then bent and wedged
into place. When all of the broken ribs had been replaced we began the difficult job of putting on the new

planking. Cold weather is a bad time for such work, for planks are brittle and crack easily.

The days went by, and though the work on the *Vanguard* went slowly, we were getting it done. On the last day of February, Pap and I finished caulking and filling the seams; on the next twenty-foot tide we floated the *Vanguard* off her cradle and anchored her out in the harbor. For the next few days we had to pump a considerable amount of water from her, but as the new and dried-out planking soaked up and swelled, the seams tightened and stopped leaking altogether. Pap and I were extremely proud of our work.

A few days later the weather turned warm, and there was the feel of spring in the air—premature, we knew, but still it was there. One morning Pap said to Ma, "What say we take the *Vanguard* into Juneau for a few days; we need some groceries anyway, and I want to buy a few tools. It will give you a chance to do a little shopping, Grace. What do you say?"

"Yahoo!" Duke and Dutch yelled, and ran outside whooping and cavorting. Old three-legged Spot sensed the excitement and began chasing them.

"How long will it take to get there?" Ma asked hesitantly, for she was deathly afraid of the sea.

"Well, I figure about sixteen hours," Pap said.

Ma was undecided, but we pointed to the strait which was glassy smooth, and at last she agreed to go.

That evening we took our things out to the *Van-*

guard, including the boys' school books which Ma insisted they take, and stowed everything away. At first light the next morning the weather was still good, and after leaving a week's supply of food for Spot, we rowed out to the anchored *Vanguard.*

Pap started the engine and let it warm up, then he engaged the clutch to the anchor winch. I took several wraps of chain around the capstan, and began heaving away on the anchor. When it was aboard and lashed down, Pap threw the clutch into forward, and we were on our way. Duke and Dutch waved and called to old Spot who sat dejectedly on a rock that jutted out into Surprise Harbor, and watched us in silence.

As we steamed up Frederick Sound, ice and snow were on all sides of us. To the west, and over our stern, the awesome splendor of Baranof Island stretched southward. On our starboard side, Kuiu and Kupreanof Islands rose, blocking our vision; the icy spires of the mainland dominated the eastern and northeastern sky, stretching endlessly, it seemed, away into the interior.

As we came into Stephens Passage, we began passing icebergs that had broken off the face of the glaciers and drifted south with the wind and tide. We continued on north, and the number of bergs increased. Every now and then we had to change course and dodge one.

When evening came the sky clouded over, and a dark night was assured. The bergs would be hard to see, so we decided to cross over to Holkham Bay and anchor for the night in Endicott Arm. The Coast Pilot said there was a fair anchorage in Sanford Cove at Sundum; the Pilot also warned of the danger of entering Holkham Bay at night when the ice was bad, and we opened the throttle another notch in an effort to get there while there was still a vestige of visibility. But darkness comes quickly in this land of short winter days, and we were slowed down at the entrance by what looked like hundreds of icebergs moving slowly out with the ebb tide. It was tricky business threading our way through the ice, and I took a station on the bow to watch. Even then we would sometimes run the bow-iron into small pieces of sunken ice which were capable of damaging the propeller.

It was completely dark as we inched up into Sanford Cove. Pap stood at the wheel, and I was on the bow with a lead line calling out soundings. At eight fathoms, Pap backed the *Vanguard* down, and I kicked over the anchor. As the chain ran out Pap kept backing down until we had plenty of scope, and I made the chain fast.

When the engine was shut down, Ma breathed a sigh of relief and descended into the foc'sle to cook supper. We boys sat on the fish-hold latch listening to the night sounds: the grinding of ice out in Endicott Arm, the sharp explosions of beached bergs as the tide left them high and dry upon the land; there was the hysterical laugh of a loon, and the imperceptible *whoose* signifying that a curious seal had surfaced to study us. . . .

At first light the next morning we boys were up. We

took our seal rifles and got into the skiff and rowed to Rocky Point. Duke tied the skiff painter to a drift log and the three of us began walking around the rocky beach toward the far side so we could look into the arm.

Holkham Bay is divided into two arms: Tracy Arm, running north, and Endicott Arm, stretching for twenty miles southeastward. On the left shore of Endicott was Fords Terror—a long, narrow tide-race of an inlet with Brown Glacier at its head. At the head of Endicott Arm itself was Dawes Glacier, and less than a mile to its left, another small unnamed one. The sides of the arm rose practically straight up from the water, and icy mountain peaks, four to seven thousand feet high, stood like hoary sentinels on either side.

"Man!" Duke said in awe, as we stood looking at it all. "Isn't it really something!"

Dutch and I nodded mutely.

Suddenly, I looked down the rocky shore and saw seal heads all over the place. "Seals," I whispered urgently, and we all dropped together and began worming our way along the beach as we tried to keep out of sight. At two hundred and fifty yards we stopped at a natural rock wall and began to get ready to shoot. I took off my heavy coat and wadded it up to use as a shooting pillow; Duke and Dutch did the same. Through the ten-power scope, I counted some twenty-five seals in the water and more farther out in the arm.

A *Trip to Town*

I put the cross hairs of my scope squarely between the eyes of a whiskery old gent looking curiously in our direction, and asked: "You guys ready?"

"Ready!"

"Let's all shoot on three," I said, and began to count.

At our shots bodies splashed water as the seals dove. As the ripples died away we saw two bodies floating low, blood coloring the water around them.

"Get ready," I said, as I retrieved the brass from my chamber and threw in a fresh load.

Heads broke the surface, twisting and turning as they sought the direction of the sudden danger. *Barrooom!* Down went the heads once more. This time all of us had scored. Retrieve brass and reload. The heads were farther out the next time, perhaps three hundred yards. *Barrooom!* Two more. A stray head popped up at three hundred and fifty yards. "He's mine!" Duke said, and shot. And it was a good one.

They were wise to us now and they disappeared; they can hold their breath for as long as twenty minutes. I stood up and told Dutch to go back and bring the skiff around to pick them up.

But when he returned two of them had sunk on us. We remembered, then, Fred Manly and Irish Cliff Kilkenny speaking of the "sinkers." Some say if you shoot a seal that has just exhaled, he will sink. Other authorities claim it is the fresh water from the rivers and streams that causes this.

Dutch pulled the six remaining seals aboard and rowed to the beach where we studied them. They are plump-bodied animals, and because the hind limbs, or flippers, are incapable of forward movement their progress on shore is slow and awkward. But in the water the Pacific Harbor Seal is transformed: every move is graceful; every action a demonstration of celerity. The seals are dark-grayish and yellowish, splotched with irregular darker colors.

We were skinning out the scalps when we heard Pap blowing the fog horn for us to return.

We ate, then pulled anchor and got under way.

As we headed northward I could hear Duke and Dutch exuberantly recounting the shooting to Pap. Once we moved out into the strait the boys descended to the galley and to their school work, for they were now doing two days' work in one in order to be finished by April when the three of us would return to Endicott Arm to seal-hunt.

Stephens Passage was again glassy, and we steamed on, passing Midway Island on our starboard, Port Snettisham, Taku Harbor; we crossed Taku Inlet with Grand Island to port, and then entered Gastineau Channel. Ahead, the town of Juneau was still an hour away. It lay on a narrow strip of beach at the foot of the ever-present mountains that stretch inland. On our port-hand was Douglas Island.

We eased the *Vanguard* toward the city float, at the foot of South Franklin Street, and tied up between a halibut schooner and an Indian seiner. We boys were excited at the thought of being in a town after so many months, and we quickly doubled up the lines and kept after Ma to hurry up. But she was methodically cleaning up the foc'sle and packing our things.

"The town will still be there when I get through," she said to Duke, who was fidgety. Presently she was finished, and we carried our bags up the ramp to the street and turned toward the business district. Neon signs flashed crazily in the coming darkness, and from the bars there came the sounds of jukeboxes and laughter.

We registered at the Gastineau Hotel; Ma and Pap took one big room with a bath, and we three boys shared another. It was the first bath in anything but a galvanized washtub we'd had in almost a year—and it was delightful. There was unlimited hot water, and one could lie back and make a prolonged study of his toes, completely at peace with the world. We played cards to see who would be the first. Dutch won, with me second, and Duke, as usual the loser, last. Dutch soaked for more than an hour before Duke and I dragged him out bodily. I stayed long after Duke began to protest and cry that it was his turn.

"I didn't know that anything could be so wonderful!" Ma exclaimed for months afterward.

That evening we had dinner at a large restaurant, and it seemed strange to see all the people and hear the sound of so many voices. Later, we took in a movie, and to our chagrin it was a phony grade-B movie about southeastern Alaska. But it delighted the Indian moviegoers when it showed the hero making a trip from Sitka, on Baranof Island, to Juneau, on the mainland, by *dog team!*

On the way back to the hotel that night we stopped by a small grocery that stayed open until midnight. The grocer was astounded by our purchases until Ma finally explained that we lived out in the bush, and hadn't been to town in a year. The man nodded understandingly, then began showing us everything he thought we might have a craving for. There was fresh milk, buttermilk, sweet cream, cottage cheese, fresh tomatoes, celery, bell peppers, lettuce, avocados—and in one corner a huge pile of Mexican watermelons! They were twenty-five cents a pound, but Duke and Dutch enthusiastically began thumping them for ripeness.

We wandered on to the "goodies" counter to pick out various kinds of pickles, relishes, spreads, canned anchovies, pickled onions, ripe and stuffed olives, jars of maraschino cherries, potato chips, cheese crackers, and many other items we had yearned for.

Finally, we had everything we wanted and carried our purchases back to our hotel rooms. I think Duke's private box must have weighed in the neighborhood of a hundred pounds. When Ma chided him for spending his hard-earned money so frivolously, he said, "Only one good day's fishing, Ma."

Back in our rooms we boys began making Dagwood sandwiches with all the trimmings. Dutch and I are no slouches when it comes to eating, but Duke's appetite is truly prodigious. I've always thought that instead of a conventional stomach, he has just one big intestine in which his food pauses but briefly. Thirty minutes after putting away a meal that would keep a python in a stupor for a month, he seems to have digested his meal completely and is near the point of starvation. To batch with Duke is to get used to the sound of cans opening at half-hour intervals into the night, until at last his wrists are cramped and sore from using the opener, and he finally gives up and goes to bed.

I woke that night to the usual sound of the can opener, and Duke was sitting in a chair by the window looking down on the deserted street. He had a thick sandwich in one hand, and a quart of milk in the other; on the floor around him were bags of grapes, celery, olives, pickles, and numerous other items.

"Duke," I said, annoyed at the unrelenting sound of his eating, "people have died from making gluttons of themselves!"

Duke finished his sandwich, the quart of milk, then

picked up a small jar of maraschino cherries and emptied it before bothering to answer. "Yeah," he replied good-naturedly, "but, man, what a way to go!"

I gave up then and rolled over, covering my head with a pillow. But it didn't keep out the sound of him breaking open a watermelon. Presently I could hear him spitting seeds into the wastebasket.

The next two days were spent in getting the many items we would need in the months ahead. For Ma, it was a large grocery order, yarn for the socks and sweaters she knitted for us, buttons and thread, this and that. Pap and I went through the hardware stores until we found the tools we wanted, and Duke and Dutch spent most of their time wandering around looking at everything, buying little items here and there. They made the rounds of the drug stores and went through the racks of paperback books with great delight. These books and magazines were then hidden away on the *Vanguard* for the days ahead when bad weather keeps one inside and boredom lies so heavily on the residents of the bush.

Finally, we all went to Brown and Oliver's, the leading Juneau clothing store, and bought new woolen trousers and shirts, socks, and short rubber packs. We had learned that, although prices for clothing were quite high in Alaska, the stores stocked only the best. We, like most Alaskans, were learning that it paid to buy the best. It had to last, and you might not get back to town for another year or more.

Duke and Dutch had turned in their half-dried seal scalps at the Fish and Wildlife Office, and received three dollars apiece for them. I contacted a fur buyer and he agreed to take all the seal hides we sent him and sell them in Seattle on commission.

After breakfast on the fourth day, Pap said, "Well, is everybody about ready to head home?"

All of us were; we'd done our shopping and seen the sights, and now we wanted to go home. The town had suddenly lost its attraction. That afternoon we moved our things aboard the *Vanguard*, topped the fuel tanks at the oil dock, and then, *cheechakoes* that we were, headed out Gastineau Channel into a howling *Taku* wind.

The *Taku* in winter is something fierce to behold. This north wind whistles down from the glacier country, a bitter-cold wind that picks up speed as it draws through Taku Inlet, sometimes reaching a hundred miles an hour. I have since been in Juneau when it ripped galvanized sheets of roofing from the buildings and they sailed along the streets like giant guillotine blades searching for victims. People are sometimes blown off their feet and slammed into the sides of buildings or through store windows.

Crossing the mouth of the inlet with a *Taku* blowing and the thermometer way below freezing is strictly avoided by the old-time boatmen, for the seas that pound across the deck freeze instantly and, as layer after layer of ice builds up on the windward side, the vessel is in danger of rolling over and capsizing. But we did not realize the seriousness of such a crossing— until it was too late to turn back.

When we left the protection of the Gastineau Channel and began to cross the mouth of Taku Inlet, the cold wind was on our port beam and, as the seas smashed savagely against the hull, the spray flew over the boat and froze instantly. By the time we reached the halfway point the wind was gale force and Pap and I were worried. To turn around and head back to Juneau would not help, so we decided to go on and hope we could make it to Taku Harbor before the ice piled up on the port side of the *Vanguard* and put us in danger of capsizing. We tried to appear unconcerned, for Ma was terrified as the *Vanguard* laid over on its side each time a mammoth sea hit.

Finally, we reached the point where we could change course a bit, and now the wind and sea hit the *Vanguard* on her port quarter. This was the first time we had had her in a storm, and now we found she rolled abominably with a quartering sea. Water rushed in through the scuppers and ran across the back deck as she rolled her guards under.

Pap had the engine running at quarter-throttle and, as we watched the ice build up on our windward side, we wondered if we would ever make it.

A *Trip to Town*

We inched up on the light at the entrance to Taku Harbor, and gradually the sea eased a bit. I was certainly relieved when we finally turned around the rocky point and entered the relatively calm harbor. We tied up at the float of the cannery and while Ma made a fresh pot of coffee and put away all the things that had broken loose below, we all went on deck and began to chop loose the ice that had us listing badly to port.

Although the wind whistled from the mountain passes at gale force, we felt secure with a good dock to tie to.

The *Taku* continued for the next seven days, a savage, bitter-cold wind of gale force that whipped down Stephens Passage like something possessed. With the glasses we could see the big combers rolling out in the strait, and although we were impatient to get home, we knew that we had better wait for calmer weather. Patience, we were learning, was the tenor of life in this country.

On the eighth day the wind abated temporarily and we headed for Windham Bay. We laid there another five days as the *Taku* began blowing once more. When at last it calmed enough to travel, we headed across Stephens Passage and barely made the anchorage at Gambier Bay. Two days later we crept into Cannery Cove at Pybus Bay, where we laid another week when the wind shifted to a howling southeaster.

Duke and Dutch had their schoolwork to keep them

(121)

occupied, but the time went slowly for the rest of us. We had read everything on board by now, and I spent the short days tramping the wind-swept beaches looking for drift, or hunting for a stray seal. At night we would play cards or read, while Ma knitted.

On the seventh morning in Pybus Bay, the wind moderated, and we pulled anchor and made a run for home. That afternoon we pulled into Surprise Harbor, and we boys stood on the bow anxiously looking for Spot. And then he came, running along the beach to meet us, ribs showing and gaunt, barking joyously that we had at last come home. I felt a lump rise into my throat. Was there anything more loyal than a dog?

It had taken us two days to make the trip to town— and twenty-one to make it back. As we unloaded our gear into the skiff and began rowing ashore, I began to wait for Pap's understatement concerning the trip. I wasn't disappointed, for he said philosophically: "Well, we learned something about winter travel in this country, I guess."

9
THE
SEAL HUNTERS

On April third the boys finished their school year and
mailed off the final tests. The following day was spent
in reloading all of the empty .220 brass, and the day
after that we began to sight in our seal rifles. All day

long we shot and experimented on the sandy beach in front of the house, until Ma complained of her ears ringing.

Judging distance is important in any kind of hunting, but in seal hunting it is all-important. The .220 Swift has a fairly flat trajectory, and when sighted in at three hundred yards, it will be shooting, say, one and a half inches high at a hundred fifty yards, and at four hundred yards it will be about three inches low. Moreover, each rifle shoots just a little differently, and it takes a good deal of experimenting with various loads to find what works best for you personally. But once you have your rifle shooting where you want it, and doing it consistently, then the distance judging comes in. And judging distance on the water is an art. Say a seal pops his head up for air suddenly at two hundred sixty yards. You must know instantly how far away he is, and where to put your cross hairs; and if there is a chop on the water you must try and make an adjustment for that as well, since only the eyes and sloping forehead offer a target.

When we were all satisfied with the way our rifles were shooting, we began to row our things out to the *Resolute*: groceries, changes of clothing, bedding, five hundred pounds of salt that we had brought back from Juneau for salting down the sealskins. Last of all went our precious rifles in padded cases, shooting pillows, and reloading equipment. When everything was aboard we said good-by to Ma and Pap, then ran the *Resolute* around the peninsula to the cannery and took on fuel. We bought several tins of Blazo for our lanterns and gas pressure stove, and filled the big water barrel lashed on the back deck.

We waved to Bill Brown, the cannery watchman, and steamed out of Murder Cove, skiff and outboard in tow, northward bound.

Frederick Sound was dead calm and our little twenty-five-horsepower Universal engine pushed us along at a steady five knots. Duke and Dutch were exuberant; they were through with the cursed school for a few months, and the prospects of a month of seal hunting delighted them.

We had gotten a late start, and it would be too much to try and make Endicott Arm before dark, so we ran into the small anchorage at Last Chance. There were some seals in the harbor, and Duke and Dutch took the skiff and went ashore. They set up their stand some five hundred yards from where the *Resolute* was an-chored, and just before dark they began to shoot. Every now and then the sound of a shot would come across the water; then as I began supper I heard the outboard motor start and I knew they were picking up the seals.

They had six seals when they came in, one a mam-moth oldster they couldn't get into the skiff and had to tow behind. I rigged a block-and-tackle and we lifted him up onto the back deck of the *Resolute* for skinning. He was the largest seal we had ever seen, and I thought he might weigh around three hundred pounds.

While I finished supper the boys sharpened their skinning knives and started on the seals. By the time I called them to eat they had three skinned. Duke said: "How about liver and onions for tomorrow night?"

"Sure," I said, and he opened up the rib cage of one of the younger seals and took out the liver. I washed it and put it in a pan of cold salt water for the night.

The boys rolled the skinned carcasses overboard and washed up. As we sat at the table eating, Dutch said, "You know, it kinda bothers me—all this killing. Ever bother you guys?"

I finished a plate of venison stew, and helped myself to more from the Dutch oven. "I guess it bothers everybody at one time or another. Sometimes I get to thinking about it, and I'm almost on the verge of never killing another living thing."

"You don't think much about killing a brownie, because he will kill *you*, if you're not careful," Duke said. "But the first moment when I walk up to a buck that I've killed, I feel real bad. . . ."

This was the kind of talk that bothers every man who has ever hunted, I thought. Instinctively, we are killers; and even the cavemen apparently did not worry about it. But the more intelligent we become the more it bothers us. And where is a man to put the blame? Haven't we always been meat eaters? And aren't the people that sit down to a Thanksgiving dinner just as guilty as the man that stuck an ice pick into the throat of their turkey? And the people that buy food for their pets—how many of them stop to think about the wild horses slaughtered specifically for this market; they wouldn't go out and shoot a horse to feed to their pet, but they're willing to buy the meat if someone else will shoot it. And how guilty are the women that create a market for mink fur? Have they any idea of the torment a mink goes through in a trap before he finally dies or chews off a leg to set himself free? And, if they knew, would they care?

I pushed these questions into the farthest corner of my mind, for there are no answers to them, and they are dangerous to a man who must live off the land. . . .

"The only thing I can't stand is senseless killing," I said. "Like someone shooting a sea gull or squaw duck just to see how his rifle is shooting, when he could just as well use a target."

"Look at Bell, in Africa," Duke said, "he killed over a thousand elephants just for their ivory. I wonder if he ever thought about it?"

"Sure, he thought about it."

But now Dutch turned the subject away with another question. "How much do you think we'll get for the hides?" he asked.

"There's not much market for them," I said, "and most of the bounty hunters don't consider them worth skinning. But I figure we can skin them at night after we're through hunting for the day, and whatever we get will be just that much more."

"But how much do you think we'll get?" Dutch persisted.

"Maybe we'll average two dollars a skin," I said.

"With the bounty, that'll make an even five dollars a seal," Dutch said. "If we get a thousand seals—that would make five thousand dollars!"

"Whoa, now!" Duke said. "Fred Manly and Irish Kilkenny didn't even get that many last year—and they're experts."

"That's right," I said. "We've got a lot to learn. And remember that they figure forty per cent are sinkers."

After supper, Duke and I finished skinning the remaining seals while Dutch did dishes. We did not have to flesh them, but we skinned them carefully, leaving as little fat on the hides as possible. Then we spread them out on deck, flesh side up, salted them liberally, and rolled them tightly for storage in the hold.

At five o'clock the next morning we were up. We ate a big breakfast of homemade sausages and eggs, and were soon ready to pull anchor and get under way. It was amazing how fast the days were lengthening. On January first, the sunrise had been at nine-forty; now in April it was around six o'clock.

The day was again clear, the sea calm. We headed up Stephens Passage full of enthusiasm; if all went well we should be anchored up in Sanford Cove by noon and have the rest of the day to hunt.

As we neared the mainland we began threading our way among the icebergs. They came in every conceivable size and shape. One in particular looked almost identical to a monstrosity I had seen in a recent *Time* magazine, labeled: "Woman." It rose perhaps twenty feet out of the water to what some warped mind might think of as ponderous overhanging buttocks, then to a narrow waist, and on to the breasts. One of these was small and immature, the other a pendulous thing that hung to the waist. It had no head, but then such art objects do not necessarily need them. I looked at "Woman" from every angle as we steamed by, but without the art section of *Time* to tell me what it was I'd have passed her up without recognition.

As we went on, the thought occurred to me that the bergs we were now encountering had more than likely been forming on the back side of a glacier long before the time of Christ. Slowly, relentlessly, the glacier had crept downward and its face broke eventually into individual icebergs that were soon lost to the persistent sea. The sun touched their many facets, and the age-old ice was the deep blue of a precious gem. The sea had washed out huge caverns in some; others, like "Woman," were sculptured by the elements into weird shapes that would have delighted the modern artist.

The mouth of Holkham Bay was almost solid with

bergs, and at times we would come to a dead end of ice and be forced to go back and find a new channel. It was nearly three o'clock when at last we dropped the anchor in Sanford Cove.

It was too late to do much before dark, but we decided Dutch and I would walk the beach for a ways, and if Duke heard shots he would come with the skiff to retrieve our seals.

In the same rocky bight where we had killed the seals on our way to Juneau, we found twenty or thirty more.

Dutch and I made a careful stalk, then set up our shooting pillows and shot together. Water splashed all over the bight as the remaining seals dove. We began to shoot independently as heads would appear.

"He's mine!"

"Take him."

Barrooom!

"There's one!"

"How far?"

"I'd say three-twenty. Take him."

Barrooom!

"Did I get him?"

"Yeah, I can see him floating."

And then there were no more heads to be seen. Out of eight seals killed we could see only four floating. We heard the sound of the outboard motor, and presently we could see Duke coming. He went directly to the floating seals and pulled them aboard.

The bright red spots of their blood on the water had begun to dissipate, but still they could be seen. Duke picked up the oars and rowed to one. "I see him!" he yelled, and took out the twelve-foot pole we had lashed a gaff hook to. "He's floating about six feet under the surface."

Duke hooked the seal and brought it to the surface, then grabbed it by the flippers and pulled it into the skiff. The next two blood spots proved unfruitful, but the last one was closer to shore and Duke was just able to reach to the seal that lay on the bottom.

"Six out of eight," Dutch said, as Duke rowed toward the beach to pick us up.

"I think we'll find this just about like anything else," I said. "We'll have good days, and bad days—sometimes we'll lose more than we retrieve."

As the days went by we fell into routine. Up and have breakfast before daylight, then fill the outboard motor with gasoline, load our shooting equipment aboard, and be off. We had learned a lot. Two of us always shot, with the third standing by in the skiff, ready to race up as soon as it was over. In this way we saved quite a few "sinkers." We rotated so that each one of us took his turn in the skiff. Naturally we were competing with each other, and my age seemed to give me little advantage. Dutch, at fifteen, was a dead shot, and Duke and I had to hump to keep abreast of his score. The days seemed never to hold enough hours,

for we were busy from daylight until long after dark.
When we at last had our hides taken care of at night,
we'd put on a pot of coffee, bolt the reloading tool to
the table and reload our brass, then make our plans for
the following day.

As we began to work our way up Endicott Arm toward the glaciers themselves, we ran into more and
more seal, but they became more difficult to get now.
They were wary, and it was hard to get within range.
Where we'd been having a lot of shots at a hundred
fifty to two hundred yards, we were now making shots
up to four hundred yards. Sometimes these long shots
paid off, sometimes not. A seal at three hundred yards
was usually a dead seal. But at four hundred yards we
often missed; it was just too far for the Swift to shoot
consistently.

One night as we were skinning, Duke pointed to a
heavy-bodied female and said, "Say, when do they
pup?"

"May and June, isn't it?" I said. "Let's open her up
and take a look."

Duke slit open the abdominal cavity, and sure
enough, there was a pup.

Then I remembered the fur buyer in Juneau telling
me that the unborn-seal pelts were worth about three
times as much as the adult pelts. We took the baby
seal out and looked at it. It was cream-colored, and the
pelt was more fur-like than that of the adult seal.

"You remember what Fred Manly said about saving a pup," Dutch said excitedly, "if you catch it at the right time?"

"Yeah, I remember," Duke said.

Several days went by, then one morning Duke shot a female that was lying up on the rocky beach. As we walked up to her we saw vigorous movement in her belly. It was obvious that she was about to give birth.

I looked at the Dutchman who for days had talked of nothing but getting a seal pup for a pet. "Herr Doktor," I said, "my illustrious brother, the Duke of Endicott Arm, and myself bow to your superior knowledge and experience in Caesarean section." I took my razor-sharp skinning knife from its sheath and held it out to him.

The Dutchman looked pretty green around the gills. "What—what . . . how do you go about it?"

"Well, open her up and let's have a look," I said. "But be careful!"

Dutch bent over the dead mother seal and made a two-foot slit in her belly. Duke and I carefully put our rifles down and moved in to help.

"I can see him wiggling!" Dutch said.

"Slit open that bag," I said, "now, that membrane!" And when it was done I reached in and lifted out the squirming little creature. Duke was ready with a piece of string, and we tied off the umbilical cord and severed it with the knife. The baby seal was perhaps twenty-four inches long, and we guessed its weight to be close to twelve pounds. It was complete with whiskers and flipper nails. The big eyes were so black that the pupils were indistinguishable.

"We got to get him back to the boat," Dutch said, and began to get out of his coat. He took off his wool shirt, put his coat back on, then wrapped the seal pup in the shirt. "Let's go!" he said urgently. "We can't take any chances with this fellow!"

On the way back in the skiff a hoarse little bark came every now and then from the shirt-wrapped bundle that Dutch held.

"What on earth are we going to feed him?" Dutch asked when we arrived at the boat.

"Canned milk," I said, "what else?"

"I know that much," Dutch answered stiffly, "but how?"

He had a problem there all right. While Dutch rubbed the pup dry, Duke and I looked for some means of transferring canned milk into it. Our problem was at last resolved when we ran across a thin rubber fishing glove. We cut a finger from the glove and, using a syrup bottle for milk, tied the finger tight over the neck of the bottle. Dutch punched holes in the end of the rubber finger, and promptly stuck it into the seal pup's mouth.

Having been so abruptly abducted from his nice warm womb, the seal pup had peered warily around the *Resolute's* cabin, now and then giving out a hoarse little half-bark, half-wail. But when Dutch stuck the makeshift baby bottle into his mouth his reaction was instinctive.

We named him Enrico, and since he knew no other parents he depended upon us from the start. Although we all fed and played with him, he definitely belonged to Dutch when he messed on the floor. And he presented another problem too; when we all started to leave him one day to go hunting, he raised such a noise we were forced to take Dutch back. This seriously cut into our daily take, for one of us had to stay with Enrico.

Near the end of April we had worked our way up Endicott Arm, and were shooting right off Dawes Glacier. This was some country. We were boxed in by the mountains on three sides, and the glacier on the other. It was dangerous country as well as beautiful. Vast walls of ice sometimes broke from the glacier's face and plunged in the sea to start a minor tidal wave. More than one man had lost his life here, and we had plenty of respect for the glacier.

We had begun bringing Enrico with us, and he rode the skiff with the pickup man. One day a portion of the glacier face broke as we were heading back to the *Resolute* after a day's shooting. The skiff was heavily loaded, and we had only a few inches of freeboard. Although we were a quarter-mile from the glacier, I knew we were in trouble before the thunderous roar died away.

"Lash your rifles!" I yelled to the boys, and we all secured them to the skiff. "Now, over the side with the seals!" Behind us, coming fast, was a five-foot wall of water. We carried life jackets in the bow, and the boys put theirs on and tossed one to me. I was in the stern running the outboard motor when the wall of water hit us. For one brief moment I thought we were going to ride it out, then we slid sideways and the water rolled completely over us.

Utter chaos. The skiff was floating bottom side up, the outboard motor was still clamped to the transom, and the propeller was sticking straight up in the air. Duke was in the water ten feet to one side of it.

"Dutch?" I yelled.

"Yo! I'm on the other side of the skiff. You and Duke all right?"

"Yeah. You got Enrico?" Dutch had been holding him before the wall of water overturned us.

"Yeah, he's here paddling around. You know, I think he's scared of the water."

And then he came around the skiff barking in fright.

At first my only thought was to see if everyone was all right. Now I felt the cold, the icy water that seemed to press the breath from you completely, until it was hard to breathe. I paddled to the side of the skiff where Duke now hung on. "Come around here, Dutch," I said. "Let's see if we can right it."

The three of us hung onto the keel and, with our feet against the top guard rail, put our weight to work and slowly sank one side and brought the skiff right side up. Then I helped Dutch over the stern into the sunken skiff. We had lost the bailing bucket, of course, and there was nothing left but our caps. Dutch sat waist-deep in the center of the skiff and bailed with his cap while Duke and I floated alongside.

I looked back at the bulk of the glacier behind us, the towering, snow-covered mountains that rose so high above, and I felt awfully small and helpless. *How many people have clung to an overturned skiff until they succumbed to the icy water,* I wondered. Enrico swam up and nuzzled me.

"How're you coming?" I asked Dutch.

"No good, I can't even get a start. It comes in as fast as I can bail it out. If I only had a bucket . . ."

If . . . If we only had waterproof skins and flippers like Enrico.

"I think we'd better head for shore," Duke said, teeth chattering.

"This is hopeless," Dutch said, still bailing furiously with his sodden cap.

I looked to the nearest shore, perhaps three hundred yards away. We were at least four miles from where the *Resolute* was anchored, but at least we could survive on the beach. "All right, let's go," I said.

Dutch rolled out of the sunken skiff and started paddling for the shore, then came Duke and Enrico. I lay back, tightened the straps on my life jacket with numb fingers, and then took out after them. . . .

It is slow going in life jackets, but thank God we had them, for Dutch can't swim a stroke, and Duke is little better. But in a way it is much better than floating quietly; at least a little circulation returns with the effort. How far is three hundred yards, anyway? Nine hundred feet . . . almost a fifth of a mile. Enrico there, swimming effortlessly, first nosing one of us, then another. It's a game to him, but it's life or death to us. Dutch slows down and I move up alongside of him.

"My arms are about worn out," he says.

"We've got to keep moving, Dutch. . . . It's still a long haul after we make the beach."

Dutch nods. He knows it as well as I do, and he starts off again. The icy water is almost unbearable; it causes pain as if a sharp instrument were probing deep into your bone marrow—a steady unrelenting pain that makes you want to scream. Yet there is not a word from the boys, and even at this unpromising moment I am immensely proud of them.

Ah, the shore! Seventy-five yards yet, but we will make it now. Duke is still in the lead, Dutch, then myself. Enrico sometimes ahead, then back down the line as if checking to see that everyone is all right.

Duke is climbing slowly out of the water, then stumbling up the rocky shore like a man with artificial limbs. Now Dutch, sometimes falling when his legs will not answer the helm. I feel bottom beneath me and stumble slowly after them. Enrico is out of his element now, and he barks pathetically as he tries to negotiate the rocky beach.

We've attained one goal, but there can be no respite. We strip hurriedly and wring out our woolen clothing, then put it back on. Duke looks back at the skiff, a small speck among the bergs, and I know he's thinking of his seal rifle lashed to the seat.

I look at the sun. If we are lucky we might make it back to pick up the skiff with the *Resolute*. If darkness catches us, however, there will be little chance of finding it again. Dutch and I feel as Duke does about the rifles; it is not only their value but because they are so much a part of life in this country.

But we must hurry. "Let's go!" I say. "We'll take one life jacket with us."

"What about Enrico?"

"We'll pick him up later," I answer, and we move off down the beach. But there is a frantic barking as Enrico watches us leaving. We stop and look back. He is pitiful; big dark eyes imploring. We stand there undecided. . . . Who can turn down such an appeal? Dutch runs back and picks him up. We all turn then, and trot off in a northwesterly direction, taking turns carrying Enrico . . .

The first half-mile was hellish, but gradually the terrible chill left us as circulation was restored. Duke, in the lead and picking the route, stepped up the pace, and steam rose from our wet woolen clothing as our bodies warmed. The beach here was broken and rocky, and at times we would come to a sheer cliff that blocked our path. We were often forced to make a time-consuming detour up the steep mountainside. On and on, eyes watching our footing, stopping only to transfer Enrico.

The sun was low in the west when finally we came to the slight indentation along the shore where the *Resolute* was anchored. I traded Enrico for the life jacket, and buckled it on. I would rather have taken a beating than to go back into the icy water, but there was no other way. I waded out, then began to swim.

When I came to the side I grabbed a tire fender and pulled myself aboard. I stripped out of my wet clothing and, leaving it in a pile on deck, went into the cabin and started the stove. I dried myself, dressed in warm clothing and dry boots, then put on the coffee pot. I started the engine, and when it had warmed up, I pulled the anchor and moved the *Resolute* toward a small rocky point where the boys waited.

As soon as the bow touched they jumped aboard with Enrico, and I began to back out into the bay. While they changed clothing I turned about and opened the throttle, and we steamed out into the arm. The sun was now out of sight behind the mountains to the west, but there would be enough daylight left to find the skiff, if we were lucky.

Duke had started the Swede stove and transferred the coffee pot, and presently the wonderful aroma of boiling coffee came from below. He settled it with a dash of cold water and handed a scalding cup to me. I sat there sipping the coffee, as Enrico chewed on my trouser leg, and thought of how lucky we had been today.

After a while Duke came into the wheelhouse and picked up the binoculars. Fifteen minutes later he broke into my thoughts with: "I see the skiff!"

The following morning we slept in. Somewhere near noon Duke finally crawled out of his sleeping bag and put on a pot of coffee. When it was done I got up, sore and stiff in every joint, and poured myself a cup, then dressed.

"Well," Duke said, "what's for today?"

We had taken our rifles completely apart the night before and cleaned and oiled them. But our scopes, which were supposedly waterproof, had salt water inside them. I picked up the tide book, in which we had marked off the days, and saw that it was April twenty-eighth.

"You know that halibut season opens in less than a week?" I said.

"Well, I'll be damned!" Duke said.

"We can't shoot any more with our scopes like they are," I said. "What say we head for home?"

"What about the scalps and pelts?" Dutch asked, sit-

ting up in his bunk. "I thought we were taking them
into Juneau."

"We can send them in on the mailboat," I answered.
"I think we'd better get home and begin getting the
boats ready for halibut fishing—we've only got a few
days until the season opens."

An hour later we were heading home, threading our
way through the icebergs at the mouth of Holkham
Bay. Dutch was at the wheel, and Duke and I were
busy dismantling the soaked outboard motor on the
foc'sle floor. Stephens Passage was calm as a millpond,
and at five o'clock we were off False Point Pybus. Duke
took the wheel until I relieved him at nine. As darkness
began to close in, there was a trace of the aurora bore-
alis in the northern sky. I watched in fascination as it
spread, the brilliant patterns of light moving across half
of the sky.

We had decided to keep running, since it was light
enough to see icebergs and drift logs. Presently we
picked up the Kingmill Point Light across Frederick
Sound. We passed Herring Bay, and went around
Carol Island. Fifteen minutes later we were abeam of
the Murder Cove Light. Surprise Harbor was just
around the peninsula.

Our house on shore was dark. Duke stepped out on
deck and shot twice into the air. We waited, and sure
enough, lamps were lighted.

We loaded our things into the skiff, handed Enrico

down, and then began rowing toward the lights of the house. Presently we could see the bobbing of a gas lantern as Ma and Pap came down to meet us.

"Well, how'd she go, boys?" Pap boomed as the skiff touched the beach.

"Pretty fair, Pap," I said.

"How many seals did you get?"

"Three hundred and nine!" Dutch answered, and triumphantly held up a big string of seal scalps.

Enrico gave a couple of hoarse little barks, and Ma, standing back up the beach a ways, asked: "What was *that*?"

"That's Enrico, Ma," Dutch said, and picked him up and carried him up the beach to her.

"Well, for goodness sakes!" Ma said.

We unloaded the skiff, then walked up the beach to the house. Over coffee we had to recount all of our experiences, and Dutch was busy showing Ma how smart Enrico was.

Enrico was with us almost a year. He loved to go in the skiff, and even went fishing on the big boats with us in the summer. Dutch taught him tricks like rolling over, sitting up, speaking, and jumping through a hoop. We never hunted another seal in the vicinity of Surprise Harbor for fear of shooting him when he was out visiting and playing with other seals. But one day he didn't return from such a trip and we never knew if he had been killed by another bounty hunter, or had simply gone back to his wild brethren for good.

And I don't think Duke and Dutch and I ever killed another seal without searching its face in fear that it might be Enrico.

10
SPRING AGAIN

Spring again! Buds and the beginning of leaves on the brush, and new grass shooting up through the dead of last year. The days are quite long now, and the weather mild. Grouse boom steadily on the slopes as the cocks send out their mating call, and thin, half-starved deer crowd the beaches as they nibble on the green buds of the brush at the edge of the woods. Occasionally a brownie is seen lumbering along the beach as it searches for something edible; as often as not it is a female with tiny twin cubs at heel. Yes, such days make one quickly forget the long, isolated winter and eagerly anticipate the summer.

The first of the crew arrives at Tyee, and the cannery comes alive overnight as the generators are started and the cold-storage plant is made ready for the halibut season which will open in a few days.

We have been here a year now and know what to expect. We are busy working on our boats; they are scraped and painted, and fishing gear is made ready. Finally, we move them around the peninsula to the grids at the cannery where we beach them and copper-paint the bottoms against wood bugs and toredoes.

We are ready now; let the fish come. . . .

Late one evening a light seaplane buzzed the cannery, then circled and landed on the bay. I untied a skiff and rowed out to meet it. I had expected a passenger for the cannery, but when the side door popped open, there was my old buddy, Mac.

We had joined the Navy together during the early days of the war, and had not seen each other since. On impulse I had dropped a line to his old home address in Oregon a couple of months before, telling him something of this country—and now, here he was.

"Mac! You Irish son-of-a-gun!"

"Hello, buddy," Mac said, and began handing his
baggage down to me. There were three bulging seabags, and a large wooden chest. When I had them
stowed away Mac climbed down into the skiff, and as
the light plane taxied away we stood there as men will,
slapping shoulders and insulting each other good-
naturedly to cover our embarrassment.

Finally, I picked up the oars and began rowing toward the float where the boats were tied. "How in the
hell . . ." I began.

"Well, it's like this," Mac said, "I was back home all
settled down to a job I didn't like. I'd just bought a new
house that I was up to my neck in debt for, when I got
your letter telling all about Alaska"—Mac lifted his
arms—"and here I am. Everything I own is in those
three seabags and that chest."

We moved Mac's things onto the *Vanguard* and
spread his bedroll out on one of the bunks. And I began to fix supper.

Boats were beginning to arrive for the halibut season; some were boats we'd known the past season,
some were new. The *Pauline* came in the next day and
it was a pleasure to see our old friend Ed Wellseley
again. There were the Jordans, a man-and-wife team

on the *Salty,* the *Cracker, Chesty, Lucky Strike, Midnight Maid, Anna May, Miss Lace, Northern,* and others we were not yet acquainted with. Fred Manly on the *Chester L* pulled in about noon, and still they came. By night on the day preceding the opening of the halibut season, I counted almost forty boats.

One boat was an eye-taker; it was named *Lynn,* and was owned by the carpenter foreman at the cannery who had bought it purely on speculation. It had just been delivered to him, and Mac and I fell in love with her. *Lynn* was about twenty-eight feet long, small, it was true, but she had beautiful lines and appeared to be in perfect condition. That night Mac and I looked her over.

"Let's go together and buy her," Mac said at last.

I didn't hesitate. "All right."

We went up the walk to the bunkhouse and found Jack Ray on his bunk reading a magazine. I told him we'd heard the *Lynn* was for sale, and what did he want for her?

"Twenty-eight hundred," Jack said.

Between us we had fifteen hundred dollars' cash, and I asked Jack if he'd sell her for this much down, the rest in the fall after fishing was over.

"Sure. That's fine with me," Jack said, and took the boat's papers from a suitcase and signed them over to us. We paid Jack, shook hands all around to bind the agreement, and a few minutes later Mac and I walked back down to the dock. We were so enthusiastic we decided to move aboard the *Lynn* immediately.

When we were finished I stood a moment on the dock looking at *Lynn*'s jaunty lines in the moonlight. I was to own other fishing vessels in the years that followed, but like one's first sweetheart she always had a special place in my heart.

Mac and I stayed up all night working on fishing gear, and by first light, when the sounds of boat engines came in the early morning air, we were ready to go. Pap had rowed across the bay from Surprise Harbor, and now he was moving his things aboard the *Vanguard*. Dutch had the *Resolute*'s engine warming up, and when he saw Pap I heard him say: "Wayne and Mac bought the *Lynn* last night, Pap—"

And Pap, in that special way of his, sensed what was worrying Dutch. "The *Resolute* is all yours, then," Pap said.

"Whoopee!" Dutch yelled, and began doing the Spanish fandango along the float.

Mac and I steamed out of Murder Cove toward the halibut grounds, the *Lynn*'s Gray Marine engine running smoothly; behind us was Pap in the *Vanguard*, then Captain Dutch in the *Resolute*. I was suddenly glad that I had a year's fishing behind me, for in answering Mac's questions I realized just how ignorant I must have been last spring.

As we neared the halibut grounds my old landmarks

came into view, and it was just like coming home after a long absence. We slowed the engine down to trolling speed and began to put down our gear. Presently, Mac said, "I think I have something on!" And we began to bail halibut aboard. . . .

In June the Thlinget Indian seiners began moving their families into the "row," a long string of shacks along the beach painted "cannery red." They came each year at this time to fish for the cannery, and their wives and young women worked in the cannery on the sliming and piecing tables, and the labeling machines. Some of these girls were quite beautiful. Many of them had white blood in them, and could have passed for white. At any rate they were available, and we were not long in making acquaintances.

One day when fishing was pretty slow, Mac said, "One man can fish the boat as well as two, why don't I go to work at the cannery?"

I said it was all right with me, and so Mac took a job on the rigging scow. Duke was working on the beach gang, and in the evenings after Dutch and I had dressed and sold our fish, we cleaned up and went to the dance that was a nightly affair.

The dance was sponsored by the Filipino workers who traditionally came each summer from the vegetable and fruit canneries in the States. They worked with the Indian women in the cannery, doing the heavier work.

About eight in the evening the Filipino string band would start tuning up their instruments, and people would begin moving into the recreation hall. The band usually consisted of a violin, a uke, a couple of guitars, and the bass, which was an overturned washtub with a long stick bolted to one side. A strong linen cord could be tightened to tune the bass to the other instruments, and, by moving the left hand up and down the cord as one plucked with the right, a series of tones could be produced. The Filipino string band was quite popular, and for three years in a row we were lucky to have a talented Hawaiian singer who knew all of the popular songs.

Ma loved music and sometimes she would come all the way from Surprise Harbor to listen to the band. But after seeing her three sons paired off with the Indian girls, she usually went home filled with despair over our futures. One day she cornered me and began a campaign against the Indian girls that was to last for many years and cause much bitterness.

The tribal patriarch from the Indian village, Moses Jamestown, felt much the same as Ma about the two races mixing, and the nocturnal activities following the nightly dance were conducted with the utmost secrecy, for there was always the fear that the wily old man would slip up and tap you firmly on the shoulder.

And a gnarled forefinger pointing at the guilty ones was usually as good as a marriage contract.

There is an aura of excitement around a salmon cannery during the summer season. It extends from the small, wide-eyed Indian children who drink pop in front of the company store, to the pert, dark-haired girls gossiping in their lisping Thlinget tongue as they work the sliming tables in the cannery.

During the busy part of the season the cannery is a continual blaze of lights, and the fish elevator can be heard creaking at most any hour of the day or night. The seine boats and fish-trap tenders unload their catches into the elevator which carries the salmon up into the cannery to the sorting belt. Here several Filipino sorters stand and pitch the salmon into their respective bins. There are five species of salmon: king, coho, chum, pink, and red (or sockeye).

Once these fish are sorted, they are ready to be canned; when this order is given, the door to a particular bin is opened and the fish slide down a chute into the "Iron Chink." In the early days of the salmon industry, Chinese workers imported from the States stood at the cleaning table and gutted, headed, finned, and slimed the salmon before they went on to be chopped up and hand-packed into cans. The invention of the "Iron Chink" replaced all of these workmen. The "Chink," a mammoth iron monster, is watched over by a special machinist, and the salmon go from it to the sliming table where the native women finish cleaning them beneath individual water faucets. From there they go into the machine where they are put into the cans, then to the piecing table where the light ones are brought up to weight, and on to the vacuum sealer. The cans are then put into trays and cooked in huge retorts. Afterward they are stacked to cool, and then labeled and packed in cardboard cases to await shipment to the States.

Some canneries have three separate can lines, and when fishing is very heavy they all operate around the clock, with time out for meals—and, of course, for the traditional coffee breaks. It is a time of joking and gaiety, and the fish elevator rumbles and creaks as the tenders unload, then hurry back to the grounds. The cans whirl along the tracks in the casing warehouse, and are dumped forty-eight at a time into cartons labeled: SALMON, OUR GREATEST FOOD FROM THE SEA.

11
OVERBOARD!

June was a bad month for us fishermen. There were no
herring, and when you do not have herring, the sea is
a dead and lifeless place where sea gulls wheel aim-
lessly overhead as they patrol the empty water, or sit

dejectedly on the rocky shores, waiting and hoping that the feed will come. There are no whales, and there are no salmon for the seals and sea lions, or for us. The days go by, and still the herring have not come. These are long, disheartening days and you lose confidence in yourself and your boat and in the gear you are dragging. When you are a commercial fisherman, your living comes from the sea, and you have only a short time in which to make it, so you must go out each morning at daybreak and fish until dark, then pull your gear and head into the harbor, sometimes without a fish on deck.

In the harbor there is endless speculation on the lack of feed, for if the herring do not come, there will be no king salmon. One man says the herring boats that fish them for oil and fertilizer have killed off the big schools and there are none left. Another voices the opinion that the testing of atomic bombs in the Pacific is the real cause. Still another claims that the fish traps have depleted the king salmon to such a degree that it really doesn't matter if the herring come or not.

These are sobering thoughts. And then there is the old question that forever harasses the commercial fisherman: *How will I get through the winter if there are no fish this season?*

But one morning the herring are there; they have come in the night. The sea is alive again. The gulls wheel low above the schools of fish, crying endlessly, diving into the solid masses, gorging themselves, fighting, although there is plenty for all. Bald eagles glide out from shore and, with hooked talons and while still in flight, pluck herring from a thick school. All manner of fish ducks and cormorants and sea snipe appear from nowhere. Whales come suddenly, then seals and sea lions. And just as quickly there are king salmon—big, beautiful, fighting fish with backs so shiny and dark they are almost purple.

And what of man? Are we any different from the circling gulls or shrieking eagles overhead? It is true that we have the facility to grumble and curse when the barren sea does not deliver its riches; but look at us now, all smiles as we pull salmon aboard. Look how quickly we have forgotten the long, frustrating days and weeks behind us.

But this same sea can be cruel and capricious too. She will show you her charms, bewitch and seduce you, then kill you without a qualm when she tires of the game. And she feeds on the greedy and the bold. . . .

I stood impatiently in the wheelhouse of the *Lynn*, drinking endless cups of coffee and watching the breakers pound relentlessly on the rocky point at the harbor entrance. Every now and then I checked the barometer on the wall, but it had not changed since early morning. The weather report had predicted winds of thirty-five to forty miles per hour, and there was a storm warning out for small craft. I paced back and forth, waiting, watching the combers out in the strait with the binoculars, hoping to see it ease off, for we had had big fishing the past four days.

There were perhaps twenty-five trolling boats tied to the float in Murder Cove, or anchored out in the bay, but none of them had attempted to go fishing.

I could not keep from thinking about the money out there. Sure money—if a man could only fish. After all the bad days, the fish had finally come, and now this storm had imprisoned us! What if it blew for a solid week? Maybe the kings would all be gone!

I went over to talk to several of the old-timers, and all of them said the same thing: it would be foolhardy to attempt to fish in such weather. The seas were too big, the barometer too low, and when the tide started ebbing the strong southeasterly wind and sea—it would be terrible. No, better to grin and bear it, for that was a part of fishing, they said. Change oil in your engine, or make up fishing gear for the day when you could fish, catch up on your sleep, if you wanted to, but forget about the fish for today.

I went back to the *Lynn*, but I could not forget them. I checked the strait with the binoculars again, then the barometer, tapping it with a forefinger. Had it gone up a fraction?

Around noon the storm appeared at last to relent.

The glass had gone up a couple of points, and it did not seem to be breaking on the point quite so hard. There was still ten hours of daylight left. *What the hell,* I thought, and started my engine.

When the engine-water temperature was up to normal, I began to untie my lines. Some of the old-timers tried to explain that this was only a deceptive lull, and was not to be trusted at all. But I had made up my mind now; there was no changing it. I slipped the *Lynn* from the long row of boats, and headed out the channel.

By the time I passed abeam of the entrance light, I was driving the bow under. I reduced speed, and then as I continued on I had to reduce it again and again. Big waves rose up to fling the *Lynn* flat on her side. But she was a strong boat, and the engine beat steadily beneath my feet. I kept going.

An hour and a half later I was on the grounds. I put out the poles, then worked my way over the heaving deck to the trolling cockpit in the stern. I had only two lines down when the first king hit. He raged on the tip of the pole until I thought he would break it. Then the other bow pole began working. Man! I had put my gear right down on top of them. I finished putting out the other two lines, and then began pulling.

The first king was a fighting sixty-pounder that took me ten minutes to get close enough to the boat to hit with a gaff. *Twenty-four dollars!* I thought, as I threw him into the bin.

By four o'clock I had a hundred dollars' worth of fish aboard, and was working for two hundred. I had the whole sea to myself, and smiled as I thought of what the rest of them in the harbor would have to say when they saw my catch tonight.

At six the tide turned and began to ebb. The wind picked up once more, and the big combers kept getting bigger and bigger. This was the worst weather I had ever fished in. I began to get worried. Suddenly the boat rolled so far over that a main pole dipped into the sea. That was it, I knew. Don't push a good thing too far, Wayne. Get the gear up and get out of here. The next time it might carry the pole and all the rigging away. I pulled the gear, and was just climbing out of the cockpit to raise the poles, when disaster struck.

A mammoth comber, much larger than the rest, rolled up out of nowhere, towered a split second over the *Lynn*, then crashed down. A solid mass of water rushed across the deck, tore me from my hand hold, and swept me out into the sea.

I fought my way to the surface, saw the *Lynn* lumber up out of the trough, shedding water through her scuppers. All four poles had carried away and were dragging behind her by the cable rigging. I spat out salt water and swam desperately, trying to reach a piece of trolling pole, a broken guy line—anything! But the swell dropped from under me and the next moment a big wave broke completely over me. When I came gasping to the surface the *Lynn* was sixty feet away, still in gear, engine running, bucking valiantly toward the distant shore of Baranof Island.

I was dressed in heavy woolen clothing and short rubber boots. I held my breath and took off my shirt. I got a fresh breath and went under to pull off the boots, then the heavy wool trousers. Now I could at least tread water. Before, the slightest movement of my legs had tended to suck me down. I rode up on the crest of a wave and looked for the *Lynn*. She was perhaps seventy-five yards away, moving into the wind. I looked about me for drift, something that might have been washed overboard—anything to cling to. But there was nothing. I looked at the nearest shore—some three miles away.

I came close to panicking then, as the merciless breakers continued to roll over me. It was a battle just to stay afloat, but I knew that if I lost my head I was done for. The will to live is instinctive, and now, without a hope in the world, I was suddenly determined to stay alive as long as I was physically able. There was no time for regrets; I was too busy fighting for my life. But I did think of Ma. This would hurt her terribly when she learned I had drowned. She lost my older brother when he was four, and I didn't think she had really ever gotten over it. She never mentioned him, but for twenty-five years she kept a drawer full of his things: clothing, a few toys, a photograph. . . .

I was weary now, tired of fighting. As I rode up on the crest of a swell I looked again for drift, but there was none. The *Lynn* was getting smaller now, still moving into the southwest. I wondered what would become of her. Would she finally capsize, or would she continue to run until she drove herself ashore somewhere and the savage sea beat her apart?

I looked to the east, and for one brief moment I caught a glimpse of something, then I dropped back into the trough. My heart began to pound, and when I rode up on the next wave I saw it. It was a fishing boat, and from her stack there was a plume of blue smoke! She was coming toward me. I tried not to let my hopes get up, for she was a long way off, and I fully realized the difficulty of seeing a swimmer in such seas. And I did not think I could stay afloat until she got to me, anyway.

I continued to watch her. Once she turned away several points, and my heart sank. But presently she came back on course. She had increased speed, for black smoke began to roll from her exhaust. I recognized her now; it was the *Chester L!*

Surely Fred must have seen me, else why had he increased speed? My hopes began to rise—could I hold out until he got there?

Then I saw Fred's new wife, Gertrude; she was hanging onto the heaving bow with a coil of line in one hand.

When the *Chester*'s bow was thirty feet away, Gertrude made her throw. I reached desperately for the line, but it fell short. As the *Chester* slid toward me I put the last of my strength into reaching it and swam awkwardly toward a tire fender hanging over the side. But the swell dropped from under me and I missed by a scant foot.

It was then that I looked up and saw Fred Manly lean over the side of the boat with a gaff hook in his hand. I felt the bite of steel in my shoulder. Fred pulled me to the side of the boat, and I put an arm through the tire fender. I had it made now.

"I'm okay, Fred," I gasped, "just let me rest here a minute, and get my breath."

Presently Fred and Gertrude were helping me aboard. "You all right?" Gertrude asked breathlessly.

I nodded silently. Fred mumbled something about having to gaff me; his face was white, and it was the first time I had known him to be without words. The two of them helped me across the badly rolling deck to the wheelhouse, then Fred put the engine into forward and turned the bow into the wind. I sat braced on a bench in my shorts, a pool of water forming around my feet. I saw blood running down my arm, but I was so numb I felt nothing.

Gertrude came up from the foc'sle with dry clothing and a first-aid kit. She bandaged my shoulder, then went below to make coffee while I changed into Fred's dry clothing. Fred stood before the wheel, slowly bucking into the mammoth seas as he started after the *Lynn*.

Hot coffee came then, with brandy in it. I sat there barefooted and sipped it slowly. Finally I felt well enough to stand up and move up alongside Fred. "How'd you ever see me?" I asked at last.

"We've been fishing in Frederick Sound," Fred said, "and last night we went into Chapin Bay to anchor. I wouldn't have gone out today except this storm had the look of a several-day blow, and my salmon are ten days in the ice this morning, so I decided to make a break for Sitka and sell my trip. As soon as I got past Point Gardener I knew I would have her on my stern, and old *Chester* runs before it fine. What in the hell were you doing out here?"

"Well, I came out to fish. . . ."

"In this sea! All I can say is that the Lord must take care of drunks and *cheechakoes!*"

I certainly couldn't disagree with this line of reasoning.

"We saw the *Lynn* when we came around Carol Island," Gertrude said. "Fred put the glasses on her and saw all the rigging gone; we knew then that you were in trouble."

"Gert is the one that spotted you, though," Fred said. "I had my hands full with the wheel, and she kept looking with the glasses. Finally she saw you when you came up on a swell."

I looked at Gertrude silently, and by the special warmth in her eyes I knew she realized I was incapable of putting my thanks into the proper words.

The *Lynn* was ahead, the poles, mast, all of the rigging down, but she was still resolutely moving slowly toward Baranof Island.

"How are we going to do it?" Fred asked. "We can't attempt to go alongside in this sea, besides all the rigging is dragging in the way. What do you think, Wayne?"

"There's only one way," I said. "I'll take one of your life jackets and get on the bow. Then you can ease up behind her; when we get close enough and I catch the boats together—I'll jump."

"No!" Gertrude said.

But Fred knew I was right. "I'll try and get ol' *Chester* within seven or eight feet of her," he said. "But don't jump until the conditions are right."

I strapped on a life jacket and moved out onto the bow in my stocking feet. I waited until Fred moved slowly into position, then got ready. Fifteen feet . . . ten . . . jump! I landed on the *Lynn's* heaving deck, and Fred was backing down.

Now came the work. All of the rigging had to be cut loose and I went inside and found a sharp hatchet and began chopping it. Off to the starboard the *Chester L* jogged abreast of me. When the rigging was clear I gave Fred the high-sign, and went inside and took the

wheel. I brought her about and headed for Murder
Cove. The *Chester L* took up station in my wake.

At the entrance to Murder Cove, I slowed down and
the *Chester L* came alongside. "Well, you'll make it
fine now, Wayne," Fred said. "I'll head on into Sitka
with these fish."

I tried to thank Fred, but typically, he said, "Oh,
forget it!" And then the *Chester L* turned and began
bucking out to sea once more. . . .

It is night and I am in my bunk. I can hear the sea
sloshing against the *Lynn*'s hull. Various fishermen
have been over with their whisky bottles to give me a
drink. Pap and Dutch and Duke and Mac have been
here and gone. I have had time now to react to the
experience today. I lie shivering in my sleeping bag in
a fetal position. My coldness is not entirely physical;
there is a cold fear inside of me, and I find that I am a
lesser man than I had thought.

I go back over the unrelated little incidents that
saved me today . . . the fact that Fred Manly decided
to head for Sitka at the precise time which would put
him in my vicinity when I would need him . . . the fact
that Gertrude saw me at all in such a rough sea.

My mind reaches in the past to another close one:
D-Day-plus-one at Iwo Jima. My ship was lying three
hundred yards off Purple Beach taking on wounded,
and we were having hell shot out of us from shore:

mortars and rockets, as well as heavy stuff from the caves of the mountain. Why did I decide to bend over and tie a dangling shoe lace at the precise moment a mortar shell landed on the back boat deck to kill and mangle seven men? This unthinking act saved my life, for I later found enough shrapnel in the bottom of the signal-flag bag to have killed a dozen men. The layers of signal flags had borne the brunt of it, and I was barely scratched by that which found its way through. How does one account for such strange incidents?

And what of this matter of fate anyway? Why have I been favored, when better men have been treated so badly? But perhaps I should not probe too deeply into this great mystery. . . .

I am completely exhausted, but sleep will not come. There is too much on my mind. Tonight Pap said: "This is probably the best thing that ever happened to you, Wayne. Now maybe you'll start using your head for something instead of a block to keep your ears apart."

The sea continues to lap gently against the *Lynn's* hull. Out in the bay a loon's laugh echoes insanely. A shiver runs down my spine. . . .

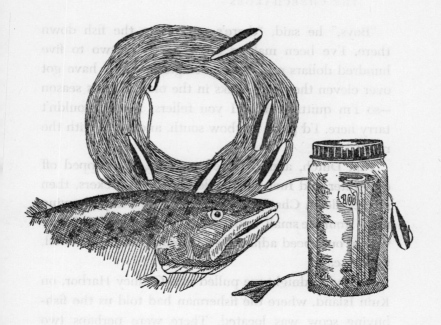

12
THE SILVER HORDE

One day near the end of July, a filthy, red-eyed fisherman came into the Tyee Cannery office and traded a thick roll of bills for a sixty-five-hundred-dollar check. He'd just come from a big coho run off Table Bay, some sixty miles to the south.

"Boys," he said, "there's no end to the fish down there. I've been making anywhere from two to five hundred dollars a day. I'm a single man and have got over eleven thousand bucks in the old sock this season —so I'm quitting. Was I you fellers, I sure wouldn't tarry here. I'd point my bow south, and make with the rpm's."

Pap, Dutch, and I wasted no time. We topped off our water and fuel tanks, filled our food lockers, then headed down Chatham Strait. Pap and I kept drawing away from the small, underpowered *Resolute*, but finally we got our speed adjusted to Dutch's and all was well, the sea calm.

Around midnight we pulled into Gedney Harbor, on Kuiu Island, where the fisherman had told us the fish-buying scow was located. There were perhaps two hundred boats in the anchorage. A great many were anchored in the bay, others were tied to the log float where the buying scow was moored. Still others were drifting as they waited their turn to unload the day's catch. We ran on to the log floats at the rear of the scow, and tied to long lines of boats.

They were all strangers, so we did not ask them how the fishing was, for that would be an unpardonable breach of etiquette. After we doubled up our lines I walked over to the scow to watch the boats unload.

I felt a surge of excitement when I stepped into the interior of the scow, walked through the crowded store where fishermen were busy getting groceries, and on into the back where the buyer, Buckshot Woolery, and his assistant weighed up the fish as the boats unloaded. The boats seemed to average between fifteen hundred and two thousand pounds each. *If it will only hold up,* I thought. *Just for another couple of weeks!*

Presently I felt a tug at my elbow. It was my friend Al, whom I'd met the previous season. He was dirty and smelled to the high heavens of fish gurry. It did not look as if he had shaved since the run hit. His hands were swollen and red and cracked, but in one of them there was a covey of fifty-dollar bills. "How's she going, Al?" I asked.

"Let's go over to the boat and have a snort," Al said, and we turned and went back through the scow and down the float to where his boat was tied. We went aboard and Al poured hot water into a wash pan and added Lysol. He carefully bathed his swollen hands, and a groan came from him. "Fish poison," he said. "I've had it since the third day. Lord, talk about fish, Wayne! There's no end to them!" He dried his hands gently and rubbed the cracks and open sores with ointment.

"I just hope the fishing stays good," I said.

"I think it will—there's lots of small feed to keep the cohos here." Al opened a locker and brought out a bottle of whisky and a coffee can. He poured drinks, then opened the coffee can and put in the money from the day's catch. "Made thirty-eight hundred in the last ten days," he said. "If I can just hold out for ten more, I'm going to call it a season and head home."

I tossed down my drink and got up to leave, for I knew he had had little rest. I said good-by and stepped once again onto the float.

As I moved along I began to see boats of many of the old breed whom I had met the past summer. Some were as old as eighty, and as colorful as their nick-names. They are the last of an era, I thought. Some of them had come to Alaska during the gold rush of 'Ninety-eight, and when they were gone there would be no more of their kind. Ahead lay Cracker-box Mac's ancient slab; it looked as if a good healthy sneeze would demolish it completely. And if Mac, whom I could see cooking down in the foc'sle, could know of my thoughts, he would no doubt charge out in a terrible rage, and challenge me to draw my big iron, for I knew he was extremely proud of his vessel, and would tell you that it was the strongest boat in the fleet. There was a rumor going around, however, that Mac was secretly afraid to put it on the grid and copper paint for fear the keel, honey-combed with toredo holes, would collapse.

On my right was One-armed Jack's little double-ender, and I marveled anew at Jack's ability to land a big ornery sixty-pound king salmon. Sometimes it is hard enough for a man with two arms, but Jack had worked out a way of taking a wrap of the leader around his stump to hold the fish up short, while he gaffed it with his right hand.

I saw the Kippered Swede's slab, Wooden-shoe Ole's boat, Coho Lars' double-ender, and Peg-leg Chris' covered skiff. And there was the *Palooka*; a mongrel boat in which there was not one line that did not conflict with all the others. But they said the *Palooka* was unsinkable, for on several different occasions she had been abandoned at sea, only to be towed into port by a vessel passing by. The present owner once told me that he was stuck with the "old tub," for she would not burn or sink, and no one else would be crazy enough to buy her.

I passed onto the *Helena*, where Silent George was sitting on the back deck painting coho spoons with quick-drying orange lacquer. I stopped to chat with him. His voice was a gravelly whisper as he talked, and his ever-present cigarette holder stuck from the corner of his mouth at a jaunty angle. I wondered if we were too late for the run, but George said that there was a world of feed: candle fish and needle fish and the small tom cod that the cohos love so dearly, and that as long as they stayed the cohos would stay. I felt better, for Silent George should know if anyone did. He had been at Gedney Harbor since the first of the run, but he didn't aim to kill himself off. Lots of people want to take it with them, George said, but that was a fantasy that death quickly dispels.

I heard Dave Matelski's voice on down the float, and

I left Silent George to his spoon painting and strolled on. The *Wanderlust* defied description. Dave was sitting on the back hatch, engrossed in taking a blood-soaked piece of underwear from his son's hand. When I asked what happened Dave explained that Davey had been in the trolling cockpit operating the gurdies when he accidentally knocked the brake off and one of the forty-pound leads headed for the bottom. At that moment Davey was taking the hook from a fish's mouth, and the leader was still connected to the line. The lead jerked the sharp hook into Davey's thumb, ripped it open to the bone, and the weight of the heavy lead almost pulled him overboard before his father could get to him.

Dave asked me if I had any iodine, and I looked closely at the open wound and at the silent boy sitting white-faced on the hatch beside his father. I went over to the *Lynn* and brought back my first-aid kit. I had Davey soak the hand in a disinfectant solution and we bandaged it. As I turned away I heard Dave saying: "Damn it, Davey, you know what's going to happen the next time you pull a stupid stunt like that? That ol' lead is going to jerk you right over the side, and when you get down to about a hundred fathoms the pressure will compress your pointed head to about this size." Dave held up his fist to illustrate. "And that won't be no fun, Davey!" Davey just grinned.

My nose informed me that Irish Bennett was cooking hamburgers and onions. He saw me and called to me to come over and have a drink. I didn't especially want one, but if I had refused, Irish would be puzzled. I went down into his bear's den, and Irish pushed fishing plugs and spoons and various other objects off onto the floor and made a place for me to sit on a locker. He put out a whisky bottle and turned to polish two dirty coffee mugs with a dish towel that looked as if it had been used to wipe the ancient engine. I quickly grabbed the whisky bottle and said: "Well, here's a go, Irish." This distracted Irish, as I had hoped, and he forgot about cleaning up the coffee mugs. I had a jolt, then handed the bottle to him. "Happy days," Irish said, and tipped it up. Irish was a rotund little man with a red face and silvery hair; he must have been nearly seventy.

Time was getting short, and I thanked Irish and moved on. As I stood on the float I suddenly knew why I liked the people in this country so well; it was because of their utter lack of pretentiousness. Engines could be heard starting up in the clear night air, and over on the shore there was the blaze of Indian hand-trollers' breakfast fires. They would soon be going out in their skiffs, some rowing, some with small inboard motors. I stepped into the *Vanguard* where Pap and Dutch were painting lures with quick-drying orange lacquer.

"What's Al got to say?" Pap asked, and I told him.

"I just hope the fishing holds up," Dutch said.

Fishermen began starting their engines in a row where we were tied, and out in the bay the rumble of anchor chains could be heard. Pap said, "Well, good luck, boys."

We went to our own boats. Dutch was tied outside of me and presently I heard the little Universal on the *Resolute* start. I started my engine and let it warm up as we waited for the boats outside of us to move out. At last they left and we untied our lines and took our places in the line of trollers that were moving out the dark, narrow entrance of the harbor. Presently we were through and out into the strait; the boats all scattered, each heading in the direction of the grounds they had been fishing. We had decided on fishing Point Ellis, a two-hour run to the north. It was still dark, but I could see an almost imperceptible lightening in the eastern sky. There was a magic quality to the night, and I felt a tightness in my chest. I wondered what the day would bring. I hoped the cohos had not left. Behind, the phosphorus wake of the *Lynn* disappeared in an unending V into the night. . . .

July. Long days of sunshine. A vista of trolling poles as far as the eye can see. And if you take up the glasses you can still see poles sticking up from ships below the horizon. And fish! I have heard stories of fish like this, but I could not believe it. Perhaps next season will be a failure, but the fish are here now, and we are determined to make the most of it.

We have been at Gedney Harbor for seven days, and we are like all the rest: machines that do the work instinctively. I have slept perhaps ten hours in all this time and I cannot distinguish one day from another. I know that I have been here seven days, because I have twenty-one hundred dollars in my Mason jar, an average of three hundred dollars a day. We are all filthy; our clothing is rank with the odor of fish gurry, but as Pap says: "It smells like money, boys." Pap and I have beards, and even Dutch is sprouting a few long hairs on his chin.

The needle fish and small tom cod are plentiful, and the cohos will stay as long as there is feed, provided it does not rain heavily for several days. Heavy rain will prompt a coho to hurry on instinctively to his particular stream while the water is high. Starting in early July, these cohos begin to move in from off shore, coming from God-knows-where during their three-year cycle since leaving the particular stream or river in which they were spawned. They average between five and seven pounds now, but they put on weight fast. In another month we will be catching ten- and twelve-pounders.

We usually leave the harbor at one in the morning, and by three we are on the grounds with our gear in the water. I am dragging four lines with twelve lures to the line. When I hit a school of fish all the poles start bouncing, and I have forty-eight cohos waiting to be brought aboard. It does not matter if some get off the hooks, for others will take their place. As the fish pile up on the deck I get behind with the cleaning, and if they are not dressed within two or three hours, the feed in their stomachs will cause them to "belly burn" and soon the ribs will begin coming loose from the flesh.

Along about noon—after eleven hours of work and nothing to eat—we stop pulling fish long enough to go down into the galley and make a pot of coffee and a couple of sandwiches. Then, back to the old grind with aching back bent always into precisely the same curve as one pulls fish. At ten—after nineteen straight hours—we pull our gear at last, and head back toward Gedney Harbor, cleaning the last of our fish on the way. But with all the boats to be unloaded ahead of us, it may be midnight before we are through.

Then we are free to tie up at the float if there is room, or we anchor out in the harbor if there is not, the three of us tied together. Each of us has a job to do as far as supper is concerned. One will have potatoes boiling, one fixes the salad, and the other's job is to cook the meat. The tender brings groceries and fresh meats out to the fish-buying scow from town, and usually we have a big steak apiece. This is something that will stay with a man and compensate for nothing but scanty sandwiches during the day.

Each of us sets an alarm clock, then we roll into our bunks fully dressed and die for an hour or two, if we are lucky. This is a vicious circle that has little meaning, but the money keeps rolling in—the fruit jar is a little fuller each night.

It is somewhere near the middle of August, and the big fishing has slacked off. But we are still doing well. One day Pap says: "We can't keep this pace up, boys; we've got to stop and rest up a bit, or else one of us will go to sleep at the wheel and run our boat plumb up into the woods before we wake up. I vote, on the first day we drop below a hundred dollars, we head for home and take a bath and clean up our boats. We'll take it easy for a few days, then we'll be ready to hit her again. What do you say?"

I look down at my red and swollen hands; I have fish poisoning, and they are as sore as boils. In the mornings I must soak them in a hot Lysol solution before I am able to work the fingers enough to untie my lines. And when I hit a fish with the gaff I can barely stand the pain that shoots up into my arm. This is actually a blood poisoning brought on by handling the viscera while cleaning the fish. It is impossible to keep from cutting and scratching the hands, and these cuts never get the chance to heal when your hands are in salt water almost constantly. Several days ago mine were twice their normal size, and I thought I would have to get the fish buyer to charter a plane by radiophone for me so I could go to the hospital. But Silent George gave me a jar of ointment and now they are better. But I am ready to give them a few days rest. "That sounds good to me," I tell Pap.

"Me too," Dutch says, and so it is decided.

On the twentieth of August each of us sells for a little less than a hundred dollars, and that evening we scrub down our boats, eat a good supper, and hit the sack. We sleep around the clock, and the next evening we pull anchor and head home to Surprise Harbor.

We steam up Chatham Strait single-file, Pap ahead in the *Vanguard,* myself, followed by Dutch in the little *Resolute.* It is midnight, but we can see quite well. The sleep has helped a lot and I am alert; but every part of my body cries for more rest. I drink black coffee as I steer, and think of the past six weeks. In some respects it seems like a lifetime. But there is a good feeling about it, and it is not only because of the pile of money we made; it is because we did a tough job and held out with the best of them.

On either side of us the dark mountains rise to their snowy heights. We run on through the star-lit night. . . .

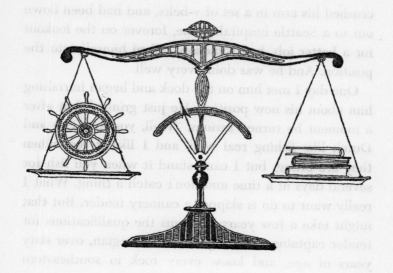

13
DUKE
QUITS SCHOOL

On our return we found that the Tyee Cannery had
had a good run of chum and pink salmon in their fish
traps, and the cannery had been operating around the
clock. The engineer who operated the generators had

(179)

crushed his arm in a set of v-belts, and had been flown out to a Seattle hospital. Duke, forever on the lookout for a better job, had somehow talked himself into the position. And he was doing very well.

One day I met him on the dock and began hurrahing him about his new position. He just grinned, but after a moment he turned serious. "Well, you and Pap and Dutch like fishing real well, and I like it too, when they are biting, but I can't stand it when you fish for several days at a time and don't catch a thing. What I really want to do is skipper a cannery tender. But that might take a few years; it seems the qualifications for tender captains are that you be Norwegian, over sixty years of age, and know every rock in southeastern Alaska. . . ."

After several days of resting up, Pap and Dutch and I decided to try our luck around Tyee, and right off we began catching cohos. It wasn't the big fishing we'd had at Gedney, but it was steady. Moreover, there were not many boats fishing around this part of the country and consequently we didn't have to wait in line at night to sell our catch.

We continued to fish there until the season closed near the end of September. By this time the equinox was upon us once more, and after a long, hard season of daylight-until-dark fishing we were more than ready to quit for the year.

By October first, the cannery crews had everything

put away for the winter; shortly afterward they all left for the States, and Mac and Duke came home to Surprise Harbor.

It had been a good season for all of us. Since Mac and I were partners in the *Lynn,* we paid all the debts and gear bills against the boat, took out enough for income tax, then split the net and his earnings evenly. We had all bought new rifles, and now with winter meat to think of once again, we set out each morning to hunt the high ridges where the big bucks were. Mac had his first deer to kill, and he was especially anxious to get a brown bear. Such desires were not hard to fulfill in this country, and it was not long before he had both.

By November we had our winter meat put up, and several deer hung in our woodshed. But for some reason I did not look forward to the winter. Perhaps it was partly because of the Indian girls who no longer inhabited the "row" at the Tyee Cannery, or maybe it was the money in my pockets that was burning a hole waiting to be spent. More likely it was just the vital juices of young manhood rebelling at the thought of another long winter of isolation, of walking the lonely beaches, of listening to the savage wind howl down between the deserted cannery buildings that had been alive such a short time ago but which now were dead and lifeless until spring should come once again.

At any rate, Mac and I began talking of taking the

Lynn into Juneau for a while. And, as we made our plans, the rebellion came. "I'll be damned if you guys are going off to town and leave me behind!" Duke said one day.

"Well, what about school?" I asked, for his books had just come in the mail.

"Who needs school!" Duke cried vehemently.

I knew how he felt, but I wasn't going to encourage him. He'd have to work it out with Ma.

That evening, just as Mac and I made ready to leave for Juneau, Duke made it plain to Ma that he was through with school and that he was going to town with Mac and me.

Ma tried her best to talk him out of it, but Duke refused to listen. At last she turned to Pap, who had sat through the whole thing reading a book, or at least pretending to be doing so. "Walter," she said, knowing very well from past experience that he would be of little help to her.

Pap put down his book and took off his reading glasses. "Yes, Grace."

"I want you to tell Duke that he must stay here and finish this last year of high school."

Pap lit a cigarette and tilted his chair back against the wall. He stared profoundly at the ceiling for so long I began to wonder if he would ever answer. "What do you plan on doing in the future, Duke?" he asked at last.

"Well, I want to live out here in the bush where a man has some freedom. I want to hunt and trap in the winter, and I figure on working at the cannery during the summer fishing season and learning as much as I can. But eventually I want to captain a cannery tender, Pap. That's what I really want to do."

Pap thought about it for a while, smoking silently. Finally he said, "I've always thought that when a boy started earning his own way, he should be his own man. I'm not going to tell you to stay here and go to school if you don't want to. Grace," he said, turning to pacify Ma, "this is a different world out here; we live by much different standards. Ability is what counts, not a diploma. Duke wants to skipper a cannery tender, so he'll have to get a job as deckhand and work his way up. Some of these tendermen are illiterate, but they know this country like the palm of their hand. They can sniff the air and tell when it's going to blow even before the barometer starts to drop. They know how to work the tides to their advantage, and they know their boats and engines, and just how much they can expect from them. These things you do not learn from books."

"But he's only seventeen!" Ma cried. "He'll go to town and run around with those Indian girls that hang around the bars—" Ma broke off, unable to go on.

"Very likely," Pap said with a trace of a smile.

"And he'll spend all of his hard-earned money!"

"That, too, is his business. He's a man now. We can't run his life for him. When I was seventeen I was fighting Germans at a place called Belleau Wood; at about the same age Wayne was at Iwo Jima and Okinawa...."

Ma said nothing for a long time. Finally she got up and began to fix supper. "I'll need water," she said to no one in particular.

Duke met my eye, and I winked. We got the water buckets and went outside into the coming night. As we went down toward the creek, Duke suddenly broke into a long-legged run, whooping and yelling and jumping all the down timber alongside the trail. . . .

Six weeks later we were all broke. Outside of a gasoline-powered washing machine that we had bought for Ma and sent out on the mailboat, we had little but memories to show for the money spent.

Duke had somehow talked his way into a job on a surveying gang bound for Seward. He'd be back in the spring. Mac went to work in a welding shop in Juneau, and since he hadn't cared too much for the lonely fisherman's life, I agreed to pay him for his share of the *Lynn* at the end of the coming season.

I was standing on the dock at the small boat harbor one bitter-cold winter day, wondering if there was enough gasoline left in the *Lynn's* fuel tanks to get me back to Surprise Harbor. I had decided that I'd collect my seal rifle and bounty-hunt until spring.

As I stood there I saw a boat coming slowly in past the breakwater. It was the mailboat, *Yakobi*. She was covered with ice, and listing badly to one side. As the boat eased into the float I saw that ice completely covered the pilothouse. Walt Sperl was navigating from a four-inch hole where one of the windows should have been.

"We're frozen in, boys," he called to several of us that had gathered to stare at the ice-laden vessel. "Could you get some lines somewhere to tie us up, then borrow a couple of axes from the harbormaster and chop the ice from around one of the doors, so we can get out."

It was a half-hour before we had the ice clear so Walt and his deckhand could come out. Walt just grinned when some of the old boatmen started kidding him, but his deckhand was terrified. He hurriedly packed his sea bag, then without a word to anyone, went up the ramp to the dock.

"Took us ten days this trip," Walt said over coffee a few minutes later. "Sure mean weather." He looked at me suddenly. "Say, what are you doing now, Wayne?"

"Nothing."

"How about making a few trips with me? I pick up a green man in town, and he wants to quit before we get across Taku Inlet. What do you say?"

"When do you want me to start?" I asked.

"Soon as we finish our coffee. We'll unload, take

aboard the outgoing mail, move over to the Alaska Steamship dock and load freight, then top off the fuel tanks and be off. I'm a week behind. Okay?"

"What about all this ice?" I said.

"Oh, yeah," Walt said. "Maybe you better chop the worst of it while I take the incoming mail up to the post office."

"All right," I said, wondering what I was letting myself in for. . . .

14
MAILBOAT

The mailboat, *Yakobi*, is fifty feet long, narrow of beam, with high bulwarks forward to throw back the seas. She has a galley on deck, just behind the pilothouse, and up forward in the foc'sle there are eight bunks for

the passengers she occasionally carries. She was built
in the twenties for government service on the Bering
Sea. Actually the *Yakobi* is much too small for the
prodigious amount of work she does, but she does it
with heart and pride. She is still on the run she knows
so well, and at the wheel is the same tall man with the
soft voice and easy smile. . . .

Loaded down with mail, groceries, machinery parts,
and a deck-load of gasoline and oil drums, we headed
the *Yakobi* out Gastineau Channel and began to cross
Taku Inlet to the first stop, Taku Harbor. The wind was
from the southeast at twenty-five knots, and beginning
to increase.

We dropped mail and groceries at Taku Harbor for
the legendary Tiger Olson, who wrote poetry and
solemnly told me a wild tale of having seen the Devil
himself on the beach near his shack a few days before.
I couldn't decide if he was pulling my leg, or was just a
little "bush happy," which is a common ailment among
elderly bachelors who have spent so many years alone.

Windham Bay was the next stop. The head of the
bay froze over during the coldest weather, and we
broke a mile of thin ice with the ironbark-sheathed
Yakobi before tying up at Stan and Edna Price's float
to unload. Bert Calhoun, who lived close by, was there
with the Prices to take our lines. I had met Bert the
year before, and he greeted me warmly. We unloaded

mail and freight, then after the customary coffee break with the Prices we untied and headed the *Yakobi* back through the broken ice of the bay.

The next stop was near the mouth of Windham Bay, where the two Carlson brothers logged. They came out from shore to meet us in a huge, flat-bottomed, river skiff. We gave them their mail and groceries, and began to unload drums of gasoline and diesel oil for their light plant and Caterpillar. I doubt if either of the brothers weighed two hundred pounds, but I think they were the strongest men I've ever known. Walt and I would tilt a four-hundred-fifty-pound drum of diesel oil up onto the gunnel and balance it; then, one of the Carlsons would grab it, roll it down his braced leg and set it on end into the skiff. I'd never seen anything like it.

Sawyer's Landing was next, then out into Stephens Passage again, Entrance Island our next stop. The wind and sea had increased now, and Walt estimated it was blowing forty knots. The *Yakobi* drove into it, the throttle-setting still right up to the last notch. Walt had a reputation of having just two speeds: stop—and "full bore." By the time we came abeam Entrance Island it was blowing a good fifty. I had heard that Walt was a tough man; now, when he didn't reduce speed, I knew he fully lived up to his reputation. The mammoth seas caught *Yakobi* square on her starboard beam, heeling her flat on her side until you had to hang on for dear life. Walt, at the wheel, braced a foot against the pilot-house wall as she rolled, then as she went the other way he switched feet.

When we were tied up at Otto Wilde's float in the lee of Entrance Island, we unloaded mail and freight, and then went up to the house where his wife, Alice, had coffee and sandwiches waiting. Otto, a stocky, gray-haired man, dearly loved an argument—you pick the subject. He had been waiting for us. He was sure Walt would stay the night and give the wind a chance to go down. And he was clearly disappointed when Walt spoke of trying to make it on to Petersburg.

"You don't mean it, Walter Sperl!" he cried. "Nobody but a fool would go out in that sea! You think it's nasty out there now—you just wait—it's going to get a lot worse!"

"I'm a week late, Otto," Walt said. "Got to make it up." He rose from the table and set his cup and plate in the sink. "Let's go, Wayne. Thanks, Alice. We'll see you next trip."

"I've run boats in this country before you were born, Walter," Otto said hotly. "By God, you'll drive her plumb under! A boat will take only so much!"

"Well, we'll go out and look at it," Walt said, still smiling.

Otto stood silent a long moment, then tried another tack. He knew Walt was a deeply religious man. "You believe in God, don't you, Walt? You really think He'll take care of a damn fool that *asks* for it?"

But Walt refused the bait. He said nothing.

"Let me tell you a little story," Otto said. "Years ago there was a preacher down on the west coast of Prince of Wales Island. He was running a seventy-foot church boat from Klawock to Ketchikan. Everyone warned him not to go out into a blow—but, like you, he wouldn't listen. 'God watches over us,' he said, and headed right into it. The sea beat the caulking from the seams and opened the butt joints—she sank with three crew members and eleven passengers."

Walt just grinned. "See you next trip, Otto."

"All right, be a smart aleck," Otto said. "But I'll be damned if I'll be a party to it—untie your own lines!" He turned his back to us.

Alice walked to the door with us, a fine-looking woman in her fifties. "Be careful, Walt," she said. Then to me: "Pay no attention to Otto, he waits all week for Walt to come so he'll have someone to argue with. Come again, Wayne."

An hour later I would have given almost anything to be back in the Wildes' snug harbor. Walt had called the Coast Guard station at Five Finger Light on the radiophone and told them we'd have to pass them by this trip. The station had no harbor, and the boys there have to lower a skiff to get their groceries and mail. They had not expected us in such a storm. The wind was from the southeast at seventy knots! And the barometer was still dropping.

When we delivered the mail at Fanshaw, I thought

Walt would stop, but we untied from the float and headed right back into it again. The *Yakobi* would drive her bow completely under, shed the sea as she rode up out of the trough, then ready herself for the next on-slaught. It took both hands to keep from being flung into the pilothouse walls. Walt stood braced at the helm, a tall, handsome man staring stolidly into the night.

I had tightened the lashings on the remaining oil drums on the aft deck, but as we attempted to go around Cape Fanshaw, they broke loose. I started out to see what I could do, but Walt said, "Let them go—there's nothing we can do now. The next big roll will clear the deck." And it did.

The latch on the galley door came loose and it began to bang. Presently the wind tore it off. A big sea rolled over the bow and slammed against the pilothouse, knocking out two of the front windows. Water poured into the pilothouse. Walt cut the throttle down several notches. "What do you think?" he yelled above the roar of the wind.

"I've been watching the light at Five Finger—we're not making headway," I shouted back.

Walt waited until he caught the sea just right, then quickly wheeled the *Yakobi* around and we limped back toward the anchorage in the lee of Whitney Island. We dropped the anchor and I breathed a big sigh of relief.

The galley floor was covered with six inches of water, and I got a bucket and bailed it out. Then I started the stove and made coffee and sandwiches, while Walt nailed pieces of plywood over the broken windows.

All night one of us stood anchor watch while the other tried to get a little sleep. The wind continued to whistle through the rigging, sometimes laying the *Yakobi* on her side when the stronger gusts hit.

When daylight came the wind had gone down considerably, and the barometer was on the rise. We pulled anchor and bucked around Cape Fanshaw into Frederick Sound. Petersburg was our next stop.

From Petersburg we headed once more into Frederick Sound, bound for the Thlinget Indian village of Kake, on Kupreanof Island. We stopped for isolated families at Saginaw and Security Bays, on Kuiu, turned south once more as we went down Chatham Strait to stop at Washington Bay, Bay of Pillars, and Tebenkof. Then we crossed lower Chatham to the southern tip of Baranof Island. We delivered mail and freight to the ghost town of Port Alexander, turned north to stop at Port Conclusion, Port Armstrong, Little Port Walter, Big Port Walter, and then ran on up the shore to Warm Springs Bay. Now we crossed Chatham Strait to Tyee on Admiralty Island—where the folks picked up their mail and freight. This was the last stop, and we headed the *Yakobi* north to Juneau to unload and load once more, then begin all over again, five hundred miles, fifty trips a year, come hell-and-high-water, storms and darkness, icebergs, breakdowns, or what-have-you. It took a man with more guts than a slaughterhouse to make this run day after day, month after month, year after year. Deckhands steadily came and went. It turned some to drink, some to God, and some to padded cells. That first trip I made on the *Yakobi* was a nightmare; after the storm we encountered southbound, the wind suddenly switched to the north, and on our return to Juneau we rode an ice-laden coffin across the dreaded Taku Inlet.

Having lived through it all, I never again worried about the *Yakobi* sinking out from under me on the many trips that I made on her during the next sixteen years she and her brave skipper serviced the outlying districts.

In April I got off the *Yakobi*. Duke had returned from his job on the Kenai Peninsula, and together we took the *Lynn* back to Surprise Harbor. Then I began to get her ready for the coming fishing season, and Duke went back to work at the Tyee Cannery.

15
THE TRAPPERS

Our trapping grounds ran from Bartlett Point, on the east side of Surprise Harbor, around to Point Gardener and on up Chatham Strait to Wilson Cove. Alaska has no set laws pertaining to trapping grounds, consequently, much trouble arises over who is entitled to a certain tract of shoreline. In southeastern Alaska, where the trapping is limited pretty much to mink and land otter, the trapping is confined to the beaches where the animals feed upon crabs, sea urchins, and small fish. We had inherited the Surprise Harbor trapping grounds when first we moved there, and, since no one had been trapping the shore southward of Wilson Cove, we had taken over this stretch as well.

It was decided that Pap would take the ground from home to Bartlett Point where Paul Stromgren's territory began; Duke would go from the house in the opposite direction as far as Point Gardener, and Dutch and I would trap the area from Point Gardener to Wilson Cove. But this stretch was too much ground to cover in a short winter day, unless we operated out of a camp situated somewhere near the halfway mark.

While we were considering this problem, I happened to think of the small houseboat that belonged to Jack Ray, the carpenter foreman at the cannery.

During the latter part of the war, two enterprising young ladies of questionable virtue had bought the houseboat in Juneau and hired a commercial fisherman to tow them out to Warm Springs Bay to conduct their trade. But after a bitter argument with their fisherman friend they were abandoned in Murder Cove, some fifteen miles short of their objective. They had spent their last cent in hiring the man, and now it seemed that their carefully made plans were doomed.

But since the beginning of time such women have found few real obstacles standing in the way of their goals. They decided to work the nearby salmon cannery—and six weeks later they had it made! The girls with the rouged cheeks promptly sold the houseboat to Jack Ray, called a plane out from Juneau, and flew back to town in style.

Jack used the rigging scow to pull the houseboat high-and-dry up on the beach near the cannery, and so it sat, year after year, until some of the planks had begun to fall from the frames and a mother otter moved in and used it to give birth to a litter of pups every spring. By energetic trading, I became the new owner of the erstwhile bordello, and my brothers and I repaired it and moved it some eight miles up Chatham Strait, where we used it as a trapping cabin in the years that followed.

On a crisp day late in November, Pap ran Dutch and me around in the *Resolute*. We brought all our gear: groceries, sleeping bags, cooking utensils, gas lanterns, oil cook stove, a barrel of stove oil, traps, fleshing poles, stretcher boards. It all made quite a pile when we had ferried it from the boat to the floor of the shack. It was getting dark when the *Resolute* was unloaded, so Pap pulled anchor, waved, and headed back to Surprise Harbor.

There is little idleness when you are trapping. The short winter days seem to fly by, and still there is much to be done by lantern light. We had come several days before the trapping season opened in order to get settled, tan our traps, kill some game for our larder, and to watch and see that the Thlinget Indians from Angoon, some miles to the north, did not jump the season a few days and set traps on our ground. They had made a practice of coming down the shore by boat in previous years and letting a man off in a skiff, every so often, to set traps. They would clean the "gravy" from a spot in about three nights, and when the person whose ground it was began to set traps, the best of the pelts had already been taken. Dutch and I decided that we would defend our ground with guns if necessary.

The first day, Dutch and I straightened up the shack and stowed away our gear. Dutch went hunting the next day so we would have fresh meat hanging, and I "tanned" the traps. This is done by stripping hemlock bark from trees and boiling it up in a fifty-gallon drum; into this you drop your traps. This operation puts a protective coat on the traps, especially the brand-new ones, and helps keep them from rusting. This tanning process also does away with any human scent that the traps might have, although I have always doubted that your scent really matters much to mink. They are not particularly intelligent, and one has little difficulty in catching them.

Although some trappers on Admiralty used "bait sets," we had always done much better with trail sets and found them a good deal easier. Most of the mink trails in southeastern Alaska are near the beach where the woods begin; once you have learned just what to look for, the trapping is relatively simple. At times, however, you will get no mink from spots that look "hot," and at other places where there is little sign, you do well.

On the third day we decided to look at our lines, and as soon as breakfast was over we made sandwiches; picking up our rifles, we went our respective ways. We always carried our rifles on our lines, for although they sometimes became quite heavy when we were carrying traps or animals back to the shack to be skinned and fleshed, there were always seals to be found along the beaches. And, too, we always felt better when armed. Some of the old-timers around the country contended that white trappers who turned up missing every now and then quite possibly could have been killed by Indians. Although there is outward friendliness, I do know there is still a great deal of resentment against the whites on the part of some natives. And there is no easier place in the world to "get even" than on some isolated stretch of trap line in the dead of winter.

I had elected to take the stretch from the shack to Wilson Cove, in the event that there might be trouble with the Indians. There was little sign right around our camp, but in a small cove about a half-mile away I found a section of ground covered with fresh trails, the earth littered with crab and sea-urchin shells. I was elated. The farther I went the better it looked. Dutch and I had a hundred traps apiece, and long before I got to Wilson Cove I figured I'd be out of traps once I started to set.

Back at the shack that night Dutch and I exchanged news. His ground appeared to be just as good as mine. We promptly sat down with paper and pencil and tried to figure out how many mink we should get from our respective lines. Then we consulted some of the prices quoted in the circulars that fur buyers always send around shortly before the trapping season opens. Mink and land-otter prices were up, and we had visions of making a pile of money during the season.

Two days before the season opened, a big Indian seine boat came cruising slowly along the shore. It did not stop, but there were several skiffs upon the back deck and we were sure that they had jumped the season and were setting traps upon our ground. Early the next morning I set out to walk my line, and sure enough, found my best ground had been plastered with traps. And in many of them there were freshly caught mink. I was mad as a hornet. Since there is virtually no way of freeing a trapped animal without harming it— or being bitten yourself—I was forced to kill them. This is usually done by rapping the mink sharply upon the head with a stick to stun it, then stepping upon its rib cage until its heart stops beating.

Now came the problem: to keep them or to let the Indians have them. The pelts would be worth between twenty-five and thirty dollars apiece, and I hated to part with them since they had come from my ground. Still, there's a difference between warning a man off of your ground, and taking mink from his traps and keeping them. Besides, the season had not yet opened. I finally decided to leave the dead mink in the traps, and to ferret out all the hidden ones and spring them with a stick. This would definitely let the Indians know that they were trespassing upon another's territory.

But this was quite a chore, and it was getting dark when at last I finished. I was hurrying back along my line, trying to make the shack before complete darkness caught me, when I rounded a point and suddenly came face-to-face with two Indians. They came up short, staring at me. Both of them were armed, and they had strings of mink over their shoulders. My mink! I had already decided that if I were to meet them I would take no chances, so now I slipped my rifle from my shoulder and threw a shell into the chamber.

"Do you men realize you're trapping illegally—and on another's ground?" I asked, the muzzle of my rifle pointing at the ground in front of their feet. I could see one of them would give me no trouble, but the other, a stocky individual with a long scar on his face, would be the one to fight—if it came to that. He spoke to his companion in the Thlinget tongue, then turned to me: "All of this country's trapping grounds belong the natives, and we trap *where* and *when* we please."

"That's not what the law says," I replied. "These grounds were not being trapped and when my family and I came to Surprise Harbor, we took them over." I was watching him closely now. "And I don't propose to give up this particular strip."

Nothing was said for a long moment, then he finally spoke: "I was in the Marines during the war—as a naval prison guard. I shot three white boys that tried to make a break for it. . . ."

"Maybe you would like to try *this* white boy," I said. I had them cold; their rifle slings were still over their shoulders. Nothing more was said, but I stood there watching them like a hawk. At last I said: "You're welcome to the mink you now have, but if your traps aren't off of my ground when I come back tomorrow I throw every one of them in the bay."

The sound of a diesel engine came then, and a moment later the dark outline of the seiner moved slowly into the small bight to pick them up. "Go on," I said to the Indians, "but remember what I've said. Have your traps off of my ground tomorrow!"

They moved silently on down the beach and began dragging their skiff toward the water. I stood watching until their shapes were indistinguishable in the night. Then I turned and began hurrying along the beach toward our shack.

It had worked, for when Dutch and I took the skiff and outboard motor and ran down the beach the following afternoon, we found that they had pulled their traps and left. But for the rest of the season we walked our trap lines with caution, our rifles constantly ready.

On opening day, Dutch and I set out at daybreak with fifty traps apiece. This is just about all a man wants to carry and set in a short winter day. It is exciting to make the sets, but is is not nearly as easy as it first appears. The most difficult part, of course, is not the setting, but the remembering of *where* the traps have been hidden. Set twenty-five traps in a row, your mind filled with the innumerable details of setting, then sit down and have a smoke and try to bring each separate set to mind. If you are reasonably intelligent you will no doubt be able to recall them. But after you go on and set another twenty-five and then sleep on it, more than likely you come up about five traps short the next time you run the line. And, rack your brain as you may, you will be unable to recall even remotely where the lost traps were set. I have spent long hours trying to ferret out some of these lost sets, and equally long hours in my sleeping bag at night going back mentally over my sets as I tried to bring them to mind. Now I carry a piece of old bedsheet with me, and when I set a trap I tear off a thin streamer and tie it to a branch near the set. When I have my hundred traps out the white streamers remind me of particularly difficult sets.

After a couple of days I can jerk them down, for they are indelibly marked in my mind. I may remember them for years, especially sets that were good producers.

It happened that the opening days of the season coincided with the low-minus tides of the month. The mink take advantage of these minus tides in their foraging for sea urchins, small crabs and such, upon which they subsist. Dutch and I, after checking the tide book, had made a great many sets along the rocky trails which the mink used in going to and from the low-water mark. These sets paid off handsomely.

In the mornings, Dutch and I would eat and wash our dishes by lantern light, turn the pelts that we had fleshed and stretched the night before, and then be off for our respective lines. We usually went at a trot, for it was an all-day job to run the lines and make it back to the shack before night caught us. During the short winter days it did not begin to get light before nine-thirty, and by three-thirty in the afternoon it would be getting dark again.

The first one of us in from our line would start a fire, put on hot water, and as soon as the other came we'd sit down and have a hot rum and talk of the day's catch, or perhaps how many we'd lost. Then we'd fix supper and eat—and the amount of food a man can put away after being on the move all day is amazing. After supper, and when the dishes were done, there came the job of taking care of the furs. Usually, one of us skinned and the other fleshed and put the mink pelts on the stretcher boards. The large land-otter pelts are so fat and difficult to flesh, however, we had a standing rule that a man had to take care of his own. It was usually two or three o'clock before we were finished and could go to bed.

The days slipped by and, although we had experienced some bad weather, we were doing well. There seemed always to be wind, however, first a southeast storm that blew up Chatham Strait for a solid week. The sea was a rolling, heaving mass that piled up night and day on our rocky shoreline with thunderous roars. Then, when we began to think it would go on forever, it switched suddenly to northerly and cleared. The thermometer went down as the bitter winds blew down from the glacier country, and all our traps froze up solid.

This makes a trapper's life miserable. Every last trap must be dug out of the frozen ground, loosened up and reset, only to freeze again after a short while. In desperation I began gathering moss and spruce needles in the woods and drying them out behind the stove. I then put them in a bag and carried them with me to cover the traps with. It now took me two days to run the line; and the animals caught froze solid quickly and had to be thawed out behind the stove before they could be skinned.

We had not brought a great amount of food, because Pap had planned on running around in the *Resolute* with more provisions on the first good day. But we had told him not to take a chance and come if the weather was not good—and now, after more than two weeks of storms, we were getting low. Not that we would starve, for game was plentiful, but we had run out of most of the luxuries. Coffee, mainly, and sugar, tea, flour, as well as bacon and eggs had gone the route. We were eating venison and potatoes twice a day now, and getting short of potatoes. One morning after our meager breakfast, Dutch stepped outside and looked thoughtfully at the mass of snow-covered mountains that dominated the northeasterly sky behind our shack. "I'll flip you to see who goes home for some coffee and a few goodies."

I had been entertaining the same thought for several days, and had hoped the sea would calm down enough to use the skiff and outboard motor. But no skiff could live in that sea. The only other way to get home was to cross that icy mountain pass on foot. The snow would be at least six feet deep, and we had not brought snowshoes. However, with the cold weather there might be enough of a crust to support a man. It would crowd one of us to make it home in a day, and if a man ran into serious trouble—he was as good as dead. But when you are full of young manhood you are not apt to think too seriously of the odds against you.

"Okay," I said, but we did not have a coin between us. We decided to draw straws, and Dutch won the privilege of making the trip. I fried four thick venison steaks and wrapped them; he stuffed them into the pocket of his coat, slipped his rifle sling over a shoulder, and set off at a trot. "See you in a couple of days," he called back.

As soon as he was out of sight I set out to run my traps. As luck would have it I had an exceptional amount of mink that day, as well as several land otter. It took me the best part of the night to skin and flesh these; with daylight I set out to run Dutch's lines, for he had left me a map of his line, drawn on a series of paper towels. I knew from experience that I would be lucky to find three-quarters of them, but I could reset the sprung and frozen ones, and bring back the mink that I could find to skin and flesh.

On the second night I began to worry about Dutch. All day it had been in the back of my mind, and now it was foremost. When one is alone and has no one to talk to, all manner of things seep insidiously into the mind. What if the snow over the pass had been too soft and deep for him to make it home before darkness caught him, and he had spent the night out? Could he survive the cold? It would be a great deal colder at that altitude, and starting a fire would be out of the question. And what if he had fallen and injured himself? He'd freeze to death. I cursed myself for letting him go. I should have been the one to go—I was six years older. Although he was a natural woodsman, he was barely seventeen.

I spent the night taking care of our pelts, and, when morning came at last, I cooked breakfast and stepped outside. In the light of day my fears seemed absurd and groundless. He'd be all right. It was unlikely he'd start right back; he'd stay around home and feed up on Ma's cooking. I set out on my trap line reassured.

The sea had calmed down during the night, and I was sure that Pap would run Dutch back with the *Resolute*. But when I returned late that evening they had not come. I was sick with fear, for I knew that if Dutch had made it safely Pap would have taken advantage of the good weather and brought him back with the boat. Night had set in, however, and there was nothing to be done until daylight.

I took care of the pelts, then tossed fitfully until daylight while the wind increased by degrees and began lashing the shack brutally. I had hoped to use the skiff, but now that was out of the question. I ate a hearty breakfast, fried some venison steaks to take with me, and set out upon Dutch's trail.

Luckily, the snow had not been sufficient to cover up his tracks. It was tough going, however, and I could see where Dutch had broken through to his armpits in places. By the time I reached the summit and had started down the other side, I was weary to the bone, but hurried on, half expecting to find Dutch at every turn in the trail. When I could go no farther without a rest, I stopped and lit a cigarette with shaking fingers; I was filled with dread.

Suddenly, ahead and below me I saw a figure emerge from the trees and cross an open muskeg. It was the Dutchman; there was no mistaking that walk! I jumped up and whooped and called, and the figure stopped far below me and waved back. I waited there as he continued on up the slope toward me, a heavy pack of grub upon his back. There is no describing the emotions I felt. But when he struggled up the last bit of the slope and sat down in the snow beside me, I covered my feelings and said, "Where in the hell have you been— Mexico?"

Dutch took out his Bull Durham and rolled a cigarette. "Well," he said, "I ran into a snow storm up here the day I crossed, and it was plumb dark by the time I got to Sign Bay. I shot up most of my shells before they finally heard me at home, and Pap and Duke came and met me with the lanterns.

"The next day I just sat there at the table and let Ma feed me. Yesterday, the good day, Pap was going to bring me back with the *Resolute,* but the clutch went out before we got to the light in front of Murder Cove, and we had to turn back. Duke and I were going to take the other outboard motor and the little green skiff and try to make it around today, but—well, you see how the weather is. . . ."

"How are Pap and Duke doing?" I asked.

"They have over a hundred mink, and eighteen otter," Dutch answered. "But wait till you hear this: Pap sent a few furs to Maas-Stephens in St. Louis, and last night on the mailboat he had an airmail letter offering thirty-eight dollars apiece for the mink—forty dollars for otter!"

"Man!" I yelled, jumping to my feet. "We'll be *rich!*"

Dutch grinned from ear-to-ear. Then he took off his pack and brought out two cherry pies still in their tins, tied face-to-face to protect them. He cut one in half and we wolfed it down. I have tasted a great many good things in my lifetime, but I can't recall anything better than the cherry pie that day on the pass.

I took the pack, Dutch the rifles, and we began hurrying back across the pass, the bitter north wind at our backs, and before us to the west, the low, arcing sun to remind us we had better be quick about it.

"You get coffee?"

"Got coffee," Dutch said.

"How about sugar?"

"Got sugar."

"What else?"

"I got flour, four loaves of bread, spuds, half a slab of bacon, two dozen eggs, and a quart of grain alcohol —a Christmas present from Pap."

"We're really going to live high off the hog, huh?" I said. "Say when *is* Christmas?"

"Day after tomorrow."

"Well, I'll be damned!" I said.

The next day we ran our lines and, since we had neglected them, had eighteen mink and five otter to thaw out and skin, flesh and stretch. We decided to let our lines go Christmas Day, and just take care of our pelts. It took most of the day to get caught up, then we washed and began putting our Christmas dinner together. It was blowing outside, snowing part of the time, but we were snug in our one-time house of prostitution. We had a couple of hot drinks made from the grain alcohol Pap had sent, and then I set the table. While we had fleshed the otter, a venison roast cooked in one Dutch oven, while in the other there were a couple of ptarmigan I had killed a few days before. We had mashed potatoes and thick, brown roast gravy, hot biscuits, and topped the meal off with the remaining cherry pie Ma had sent. We had hot coffee liberally laced with 190-proof alcohol, and finally relaxed with cigars I had saved for the occasion.

Several days before the season closed we had a serious accident. Dutch, while resetting an otter trap, accidentally tripped the pan and the heavy, toothed trap neatly broke two of his fingers and severely mangled his hand. He extricated himself and, tearing off a piece of his shirt in which to wrap the badly bleeding hand, he set out for our shack. He was lying on his bunk in terrible pain when I returned late that evening. His hand was still wrapped in the bloody piece of shirt, and was badly swollen. I gave him a stiff shot of alcohol from our Christmas bottle, then soaked his hand in an Epsom salts solution. The hand was a mess. It must have upset me more than I knew and, while Dutch soaked the mangled hand, I went outside feeling sick to my stomach. I lay for several minutes upon the cool snow, then went back inside and began to whittle splints for the broken fingers. I straightened them as best I could, lashed on the splints, and bandaged the other deep wounds made by the teeth of the trap.

When I was through, I gave the feverish Dutch another stiff drink and put him back to bed. I stepped outside once more, and studied the weather. It was still blowing hard; there would be no chance to take him home by skiff. And I knew that, sick as he was, I could never get him over the pass. The clutch was out on the *Resolute*, and Dutch had told the folks not to worry about us, that we'd come home by skiff the first good day after the season closed. Well, there was nothing to be done but take care of the hand as best we could, and hope for a break in the weather.

By morning Dutch's hand was swollen to almost twice its normal size, and he was in great pain. The only medicine we had was aspirin, and I gave him some, though it seemed to help but little. I had taken care of our pelts during the night while I watched

Dutch, and now he insisted that I go ahead and run my line since I could do nothing for him. I agreed to go and pull up my traps, then the next day his—if the sea had not calmed by then—so we'd be free to make a break for home when we did get the chance.

At first light the following morning I stepped outside to study the weather. The wind seemed to be decreasing, though a heavy swell from the southeast still beat upon the point. I hurriedly cooked our breakfast and began to get our gear ready. I tied the furs in bundles and lashed our sleeping bags around them. We had one hundred sixteen mink and thirty-odd otter, and we hoped to get somewhere around forty-five hundred dollars for them. But I was not thinking of money now; my only thought was to get Dutch home. Ma would know what to do. Dutch's traps were still out, but the season closed the day after tomorrow and one of us could come back and pull them later.

I got the outboard motor ready, then came a shock: our spare tin of gasoline had rusted through and was empty. I emptied both gas lanterns of their contents, added as much stove oil as I dared, and then did some calculating. Including the mixed gasoline already in the outboard motor, there was only about two and a half gallons of fuel. It would not be enough to get us home, but if we could somehow manage to get past Point Gardener, we had a chance of rowing home from there. The tide and wind would be against us, and the three-horsepower outboard would not make very good time even if the swell decreased enough for us to run at full throttle.

By noon the sea had quieted down enough so I figured I could launch the skiff. I wasn't worried about the skiff; it was a round-bottomed, Indian-built affair, sixteen feet long, and wide of beam. It would take a devilish sea and come through if properly handled. I went back inside to where Dutch lay and put all the cards on the table, then left the decision up to him.

"Well," he said, "if we don't try now we might not get another chance for a week—or maybe more. It's stormed for a solid month now, and maybe it's good for another. I'm so weak I couldn't begin to make it over the pass. . . ." He paused a long moment. "The only other thing I can think of is for you to go back over the pass alone and try—oh, hell, I don't know, Wayne."

I had thought of that too, but when I got home we'd still have no way to come back and get him. The *Resolute* was out of commission, as was the *Vanguard*. The cannery tenders at Tyee were beached and laid up for the winter. And what if something happened to me in crossing the pass? Dutch would be left alone and no one would know about him. No, it would be better to stick together.

Dutch must have sensed my thoughts, for he said, "What the hell, let's try it in the skiff!"

On that note I dragged the heavy skiff to the water's

edge. I filled the outboard motor, clamped it to the mount on the stern, and carefully stowed the remaining fuel inside. Then I carried our sleeping bags and furs down and put them in the bow. I covered them with a tarp to keep them dry, returned to the shack and filled a small box with grub in case we had to spend a night or two on the beach.

"You ready?" I asked Dutch.

"Ready as I'll ever be," he replied, shaking from the cold and his weakness.

I pushed the skiff out until the swells began to lift it, then Dutch crawled in and got under the canvas. I jumped aboard and pushed out into deeper water with an oar, then choked the motor and pulled the starter cord. On the second pull it started, and we were off.

Out in Chatham Strait a big white one rolled and broke, and I decided to hug the shore all the way to Point Gardener. If we capsized we'd at least have a chance of making the beach. For a half-hour we ran at full throttle, then, by degrees it became worse and I was forced to slow down or take green water over the bow. Several times a big one would catch us unaware, half fill the skiff, and both of us would bail furiously in fear that another big one might catch us low in the water.

As the wind and sea increased I kept slowing down, until, watching a landmark I could see on shore I knew we were hardly moving at all. Precious fuel was being burned, and yet we were getting nowhere. To our starboard, and some six miles across the strait, Baranof Island rose to its snowy heights; beautiful, cold, deadly as the merciless sea on which we tossed. And ahead was the light at Point Gardener, only a couple of miles now, but did we have the fuel to make it? If only the tide would ebb—but then the tide would be against the wind and we would be fighting the terrible riptides coming at us from every quarter.

The motor missed suddenly, picked up briefly, then died. We were out of gas. I refilled it from the can, cursing as the skiff slid around into the trough and I spilled precious fuel. In a little while I had it going once more, but I was filled with despair, for we had used much more than I had counted on. If we did not do better than this we had no hope of getting around the point. Finally, I could see that we were not gaining any ground, and I throttled down and headed for a small indentation in the shore line.

For two hours we lay at anchor in the small bight waiting for a lull. At last it came; it wasn't much better, but we decided to try it. If we could not get around the point this time we would be forced to turn and row back toward our trapping shack. For what seemed like hours we bucked into the still stiff wind, and looking at my marks on shore I could see that we were just barely moving ahead. Suddenly the motor coughed and died. That was the last of the fuel. I unscrewed the cap to the gas tank to make sure. I was again filled with despair; we had been so close to making it.

Then, like the hero in an old-time thriller, Dutch pulled the bottle of 190-proof alcohol from beneath his heavy sheepskin coat, handing it to me silently. It was almost half-full. "Cheers," Dutch said, grinning. I took it and unscrewed the cap; I stuck the neck of the bottle into the filler hole and turned it up, hardly spilling a drop. The motor coughed a couple of times as I pulled on the starter cord, then fired. We were back in the race.

Slowly we inched by the point, through the gap between the light and the shore. Suddenly we could look back into Surprise Harbor and see the house, though it was still a couple of miles away. It was a welcome sight, and we were filled with confidence.

The engine finally ran out of fuel, but we had it made now. I broke out the oars and traded places with the Dutchman. I bent my back against the pull of the oars, rowing slow and steady, feeling so good I wanted to break out singing. Dutch, sitting hunched in his coat on the stern seat, was grinning too. It would not be long now.

16
WE MOVE
TO BARANOF

Did you ever visit some old abandoned shack away in
the brush? It's a strange feeling. Whenever I chance
on one I am always a little depressed, but still curious.
I poke through the debris, the things that were left as

not worth taking to some new home, seeking information about the people that once lived here. Did they leave for purely economic reasons, or was it because the spot did not live up to their expectations? Perhaps they lived and died here, and now all their efforts seem wasted, for the place is falling in, and has been picked over by human scavengers.

For several years we were content in Surprise Harbor, but gradually we began to realize that it lacked many things, and when at last we found a better location, we abandoned our cabin and moved on.

Sometimes while hunting over on Admiralty, I stop by our old homesite and I am filled with memories. In the debris I see an ancient set of bronze gurdies, and recall all the troubles I had with them before they were discarded. I see a color photo of the Arizona desert, the background filled with cactus and a setting sun, but now the glass and frame are broken. The picture has been in the family longer than I have. Over against the wall is a worn-out pair of rubber boots, and I remember that I once nearly drowned before I could get them off. . . .

There is no house now, for after we moved away Pap and we three boys bought a small sawmill and, knocking out the partitions and ends of the building, we set up the mill and began to saw lumber. We came over periodically to cut tall, straight yellow cedar from the ridges, buck them into forty-foot lengths, and move them with logging jack and Beebe winch to the water so they could be floated to the sawmill to be sawn. It was back-breaking work to move such logs with no power except the power of your arms cranking the hand winches or working the jack, but we had a vision. We were going to build ourselves a fleet of new boats; big "smoke" boats that could take the deadly Gulf of Alaska if need be. We bought a set of plans calling for a forty-six-footer, with twelve foot of beam. First we would build me a boat, then Pap, then Dutch. Duke was skippering cannery tenders during the summer months now.

Over a four-year period of working when we had the time, we accumulated over twenty thousand board-feet of choice, vertical-grain boat lumber—enough for the first two boats. We were just putting the finishing touches on the boat shop we were building in our new home in Warm Springs Bay, and getting ready to haul the lumber over, when one of those little tricks of fate intervened.

It was October and hunting season was open. As a rule you never see another hunter in our part of the country. But on this particular day a Coast Guard buoy-tender pulled into Murder Cove and tied to the dock there. They were ahead of schedule and so the captain gave liberty to those who wanted to hunt. A party of deer hunters rowed to each side of the bay, one heading east, the other west to the ridges behind

Surprise Harbor. By night all of the hunters were back, except for a young man born and raised in the city. He became lost and then terrified as dark began to catch him in the woods. He began to run, and at last came out on the shores of a bay. But it was Surprise Harbor and not Murder Cove, and he hadn't an idea in the world where he was. At last, looking across the bay, he saw the dim outlines of buildings and began to trot around the edge toward them. When he came to our sawmill he had the presence of mind to stay there the night and wait for the searching party.

There was a chill to the night, and the boy dragged a piece of tin into the mill and built a fire on it. He found an old comforter in the nearby shop, rolled up in it, and lay down in a sawdust pile near the fire. Presently he was sound asleep.

Sometime during the night he awoke to the smell of smoke. The floor of the mill was on fire, and flames were nibbling at the pile of sawdust where he lay. He jumped to his feet in panic and ran out into the night. The mill was a roaring inferno by the time he stumbled back from the creek with an old kettle half full of water.

The searching party had little difficulty in finding their lost hunter the next morning, for smoke still rose from the burned building. The officer in charge looked at the twisted scraps of metal that had been the mill carriage, the warped and blackened saw, the gasoline-driven engines that lay smoldering on their sides, and asked the boy what else had been in the mill.

"Well, there was a shed alongside that had some lumber in it. . . ."

The officer nodded and led the party back across the peninsula.

Four men had labored off and on for four years man-handling the heavy logs down from the high ridge in order to saw and stack the boat lumber that was sea-soning in the shed, but when the officer made out his report of the fire, he merely noted that: "An old aban-doned sawmill was accidentally burned last night by one of our men. It was apparently without value. . . ."

When we petitioned for damages we learned, to our chagrin, that you cannot sue the government without their permission—and we definitely did not have per-mission. Our only recourse was to sue the boy himself, but there was little point in doing this, for what eight-teen-year-old could ever hope to repay us for all that had gone up in smoke?

But I have gotten ahead of my story. For several years it had been evident that in settling in Surprise Harbor we had picked a poor spot. The struggle to keep a full belly and just to stay alive out in this wil-derness is enough to keep settlers occupied most of the time, but there are a great many things that can make this life easier and much more enjoyable. We had come to Alaska full of plans, but after seven years in Surprise Harbor we still carried water from the creek in pails, read by kerosene lamps, and used an outhouse. Our house stood at the head of a tidal flat where, at high tide, the sea came to within a few yards of our front door; at a low-minus tide it was almost a half-mile to where we had enough water to anchor the boats. Also, Surprise Harbor was open to southeasterly weather so that, during the fall and winter storms, the sea rolled up Chatham Strait from the open ocean, growing savage within this long stretch. The wind and mountainous seas swept into the harbor, and we had only scant protection for the boats in the lee of Deer Island. During these storms we had to row out to the moored boats and stand anchor watches, sometimes for days and nights at a time.

When groceries or something from the mail-order houses came out from town on the mailboat, it was put off on the dock at the cannery in Murder Cove. During the winter when the weather was too rough to haul these things around the peninsula by boat, we had to carry them across the trail upon our backs.

We were continually looking for an ideal spot in which to settle permanently. We wanted a good harbor for our boats, and a stream with enough "head," or drop, to provide sufficient pressure to pipe water into the house. This same drop would enable us also to install a generator driven by water power. With dependable electricity we could get a deep-freezer to store game in, as well as have power for lights and tools. A good garden spot was desirable, but of secondary importance since we could transport good soil if necessary.

During the summers we explored every bay for miles around, but could not find just what we wanted. If we discovered a stream that could be turned to water power, there was a poor harbor, or vice versa. For a while we thought we had come across the perfect spot in Red Bluff Bay, on Baranof Island, some twenty-five miles southwest of us; but then we learned that the bay froze-in solid during the winters. Isolation itself didn't bother us so much, but what if one of us had a bad accident, or became sick?

It was not until the summer of 1953 that we found our new home.

Warm Springs Bay is located on the eastern side of Baranof Island. There are hot mineral springs on the hill behind the small settlement of Baranof, and it is this that gives the name to the bay. The Thlinget Indians went there long before the white man took an interest in Alaska; they went to bathe in the pools of hot water that bubbled from the rocks. In the early part of this century there were a few white people living there, and gradually more came. Soon the settlement began to take on the air of a town; there were a couple of general stores, a bakery, saloons, and several other small businesses. Eventually a sawmill was constructed near the big waterfalls that cascade down from the lake above. A quarter-mile east of the settlement a fish saltery was built and began to salt down herring and salmon in big wooden kegs, some weighing about eight-hundred pounds when full. There were quite a number of fishermen around then.

But, in the late twenties, the salteries around the various bays began to go out of business. They could not compete with the salmon canneries. The sawmill in Warm Springs Bay survived for a few years more, but eventually it went the way of the salteries. With this income gone, the village began to dry up; most of the people left, and the empty buildings began to fall down.

For the most part the remaining residents of Warm Springs Bay seemed to be a rowdy lot; there was much feuding and fighting and drinking there. Over the years Pap and we boys had occasionally stopped in for a bath or a bottle of liquor while out on a fishing trip. We came to know the feuding factions fairly well, but had no desire to live in such surroundings.

When I stopped in to take a bath that day during the summer of 1953, I was amazed at the place, for the roughnecks were gone; only a few colorful old pensioners remained. Sadie Fenton, a shrewd old lady in her middle sixties, owned and operated a general store, public bathhouse, a liquor store, and she had a few cabins to rent as well. Her partner in the business, Fred

O'Neal, had drowned the previous year, and Sadie told me that she was too old to operate the place by herself any longer. She had decided to sell out. Only last week a man and his wife had flown out from Sitka to look at it, but they had complained of her price—twenty-five thousand dollars.

I stood up and walked over to the open window. An idea began to fester in my head. It was a sunny August day, and I had never seen a more beautiful spot. There was a steady roar from the falls, and I could feel the fine spray against my face as the breeze lifted and carried it across the water. This was the place we Shorts needed. We would have steady electricity, hot and cold running water in all of the buildings, and a good harbor for our boats. Although there would be people stopping in during the summer months, we would still be able to live the isolated life we preferred. There would be plenty of room for all of us, and if and when one of us boys could ever find a woman crazy enough to share such a life—there would be room for her, too.

Although some of the buildings were in a state of disrepair, a lot of money had been spent to develop the spot. The most important thing, as far as I was concerned, was the small hydroelectric plant. Several thousand feet of six-inch wooden water pipe came down the steep mountainside from the lake above to drive the Pelton wheel, which in turn drove a four-

kilowatt generator. It is a well-known fact that water
power is the cheapest and most efficient means there is
of producing electricity. Sadie told me that it cost her
approximately ten dollars a year to operate the plant—
the price of a pair of vee-belts and lube oil. The plant
ran twenty-four hours a day, every day of the year.

Seven hot mineral springs up on the mountain were
channeled into a four-inch wooden pipe which carried
the hot water down to the public bathhouse and
cabins. It occurred to me that with a surplus of hot
water a person could build a hothouse and heat it. After
considering all this—the unique site, the seven buildings, the stock in the general store and liquor store, the
equipment and tools—I didn't think her price was too
much.

When I turned away from the window I had made
up my mind to get this place if I had to rob a bank to
do it. "Sadie," I said, "why don't you sell it to me?"

She gave me that shrewd, birdlike look. "You got the
money, Cowboy?"

"No," I admitted.

"Well, a hard-working fellow like you ought to be
able to raise a down payment. Tell you what, you give
me ten thousand dollars down—and you can pay the
rest off at two hundred dollars a month. How's that
sound?"

I said that I'd see what I could do.

"No, we can't do it that way," Sadie said. "We either

settle the deal right now, or I'll be forced to accept that Sitka couple's money if they meet my price. I'm giving you a break because I like you, Cowboy— anybody else has to have cash."

"How soon?" I asked, scarcely breathing.

"My old bones are beginning to ache, and not even the hot baths help. I got it in my bean that I'll go down to sunny California and spend the rest of my days. I want to leave here before the snow starts to fly."

"How do you want to do it?" I asked.

"Well, you give me some money down and write an agreement."

I looked in my billfold. After buying a bottle of liquor and paying for my bath I had exactly four dollars and eighty cents left. I shook it sheepishly out upon the table, and looked at Sadie. "That's the works."

Sadie, to my surprise, was not insulted by this meager sum. She picked up the bills, counted the change, then said, "Eighty cents, huh? Well, let's call it five dollars even. Now then, sit down and write out an agreement."

I sat down a long moment, thinking. Then on a piece of paper towel, I began to write. . . .

An hour later I was steaming out the mouth of the bay, homeward bound. For four dollars and eighty cents American money, I had an option to buy the lay-out in Warm Springs Bay. I wondered what the rest of the family would say when I told them. My hard-headed family didn't believe in owing money. Our policy was to pay cash, and when we didn't have the cash, well, we just tightened up our belts, and worked a little harder. At this time we had very little cash.

"Bought the O'Neal-Fenton layout in Warm Springs Bay!" they chorused. Then: "What with?"

We talked and argued for three days—days in which we should have been fishing. I used every device at my command: cajolery, humility, sarcasm, shame. I had one thing in my favor: they all liked the site, especially since learning the rowdy bunch was no longer there. But the one thing we had to agree on was that we just didn't have the money.

I realized that I'd have to appeal to each of them differently in order to change their minds about going into debt. I began with Ma. I got her alone and said, "Ma, look at us, we've been here seven years, and what do we have to show for it—nothing but a primitive shack that an Indian would be ashamed of!" Then I began to tell her of all the wonderful things we would have if we bought the place in Warm Springs Bay. . . .

Next I talked to Pap. We were walking along the sandy beach toward Sign Bay looking for a good fir-wood log that might have floated in from Canada or Puget Sound. "Pap," I said, "you know the money we were going to put into a gasoline light plant, so's to have lights in the winter, and power for tools when we get around to building our big boats?"

"Yeah," Pap said noncommittally.

"Well, if we put that money into the layout at Warm Springs we wouldn't have to get the plant—we'd have all the free water power we wanted to run table saws and band saws, planers, drills. We could build a big boat shop, and really do a professional job of it."

"What about the place here?"

"Leave it. It's no good anyway!"

"What about the small sawmill that we were going to buy, so we'd have lumber to build those big boats with?"

"We'll just wait until we can afford one. We could still set the mill up over here, and come over every now and then to log and saw up a little lumber."

Pap stopped to roll a smoke. He looked back across the bay, then said thoughtfully, "You know, we could knock out the ends of the house, the partitions, add on a little floor space, put in a ramp, and use it to saw lumber in, huh?"

"We just *haven't* got the money, Wayne," Duke said, his gaze focused on some faraway peak on Baranof Island across the strait.

"You know," I said, "if all the damned ingrained stubborness we Shorts have inherited from our ornery Scotch-Irish-Texan forebears was headed in the right direction—nothing could stop us."

"I doubt if we've got enough between us for the

down payment—and, holy cow, *twenty-five thousand dollars!*"

"So what—people down in the States pay that much just for a little bitty wickiup to live in! We'll be getting a business, some income that'll help make the payments."

"I don't know," Duke said, shaking his head.

"Well," I said, "if four grown men and one of the toughest women in Alaska can't stick their necks out a little—I guess we'd better dig a hole on the beach and pull some sand on top of us." I turned abruptly away from him and walked slowly back toward the house.

That night after supper Duke got a piece of paper and pencil and sat down at the table. "How much can we raise?" he asked.

From all sources—savings, war bonds, life insurance policies that could be cashed in, everything—we finally added up six thousand dollars.

We had our boats, but we did not dare try and borrow on them, for in the first place we would have to put out several hundred dollars insuring them before any bank would give us money against them. And too, if the next season was bad, we'd lose everything! Our boats were our livelihood. We could not risk them. It seemed as if we were whipped before we had started. We all sat in silence as the red glow of the sun slid behind the snow-capped peaks of Baranof to the west. There was nothing more to be said. At last Ma rose from the table and lit a lamp. She set it upon the table, and for a brief moment I felt her hand touch my shoulder.

I rose, picked my rifle up and stepped to the door. I had to get away for a while. "Guess I'll walk over and see Paul and Jerry," I said.

"I'll go with you," Duke said, and lifted his wool jacket from the deer antlers on the wall by the door. We stepped outside into the clear evening air, crossed the creek, and went along the narrow trail to Murder Cove.

We carried the light skiff to the water's edge and rowed across the bay to where Paul's boat was anchored for the night.

"Come in, come in," Paul said. "Put some coffee on, Jerry, the boys are here."

We talked for an hour of idle things, then Paul said, "I hear from the grapevine you boys are going to buy out Sadie, over in Warm Springs Bay."

I admitted that we had been thinking about it, but we just couldn't quite cut the mustard financially.

"How much do you need?" Paul asked politely, as though prying into business that did not concern him.

"Four thousand," Duke said.

Paul rubbed his nose a moment, and knocked the dottle from his ever-present pipe. Finally he reached into a drawer beneath his bunk and came out with a checkbook on the Petersburg Bank. He searched for a pen, found one, and slowly scrawled out our names upon the check before our startled eyes. He pushed the check across the galley table, saying, "I can let you boys have more if you need it. . . ."

Duke picked up the check and studied it. Neither of us could find the words for a long moment, then Duke mumbled something about us giving Paul a note.

Paul snorted through his nose as though Duke had insulted him. "Look," he said, "you're going to be plenty busy making those payments and improving the place. There's no hurry about paying me back . . . whenever you can do it without jeopardizing your investment."

That night we walked back along the trail by lantern light, Paul's check buttoned tightly in Duke's shirt pocket.

"You know," Duke said, "you don't find many like Paul."

"No," I said, "you don't," and there was a lump in my throat.

Now we all turned to with a will. Duke was running a pile driver for the cannery. Ma got a job washing dishes at the cannery cook house and, until it closed in the middle of September, she journeyed alone over the trail, rowed across the bay to work, then back each night—a tall, resolute woman of fifty-five, carrying a .30/06 rifle for protection against brown bear.

Pap, Dutch, and I drove ourselves and our boats from daylight until after dark. I fished a trip to Juneau, sold the catch, and talked to the man in charge of the Alaska Communication System. He assured me they would send a new radiophone out to Warm Springs Bay and have a man install it. It would cost us nothing; it was just that we'd have to keep a nightly schedule with Juneau. We would also have a mail plane once a week in addition to the regular mailboat service.

So, on the second of October, we loaded all our possessions onto the boats during a first snow flurry. Ma said, "This is one time I'm glad to move." Old Spot had long since died, and our new dog, Michael J. O'Toole, jumped overboard five times in a row and swam back to the house we were leaving. Finally, just before dark, we got him corralled in the foc'sle of the *Vanguard* and at last we were on our way.

As we began to cross the strait a little southeast wind came up; Ma, travelling with me on my new boat, the *Wooden Shoe*, began to get seasick. I realized suddenly this was the first time we had gotten her aboard one of the boats since our epic trip to Juneau almost seven years before.

But after another half-hour the wind began to die, and the sea eased to a gentle swell. The breeze soon switched to the north and the sky began to clear, with scattered stars overhead. Presently we could see the blinking light at the entrance of Warm Springs Bay.

"Tell me again of our new home," Ma said.

I began to tell her of all the wonderful things we would have there. She was silent for several minutes after I had finished.

"I hated Surprise Harbor," she said at last, looking into the night from where we'd come. "Sometimes I thought I would die from the loneliness when all of you were away in the summer for weeks on end. I've not known such loneliness since you were a baby and your father and I took a homestead on the Arizona desert. He was gone a lot, and there was just you and Lynn and me—then Lynn died."

I reached over and took her hand. "It'll never be like that again, Ma—I promise."

"I don't mind being alone, so much—I don't know how to talk to strangers, anyway. But I like to be able to see people now and then."

We passed abeam of the blinking light on the rocky shore, and then we were in the bay. I began to think of what I would do. I must find a job of some kind. The trapping season was closed this winter, and there would be no work around the towns. There was only one thing left: I must go Outside. I began to think . . . San Francisco, now, that had a pretty sound to it. . . .

We came around a little point of land, and there, suddenly, were the lights of the settlement ahead.

"It won't be long now, Ma," I said.

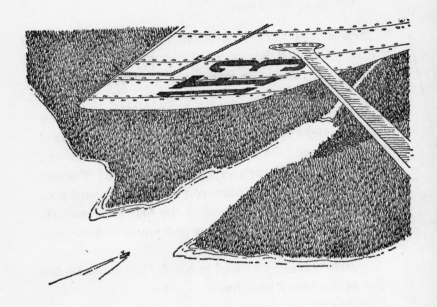

17
A BRIDE
COMES NORTH

There is no place on earth as lonely as the city, for a person used to living out in the wilderness. You may go to a movie or restaurant and sit among any number of people, yet you are a stranger and as isolated from them by convention as you would be if you lived a thousand miles from your nearest neighbor. You may stand in a crowd waiting for a bus and be more alone than on an uninhabited stretch of trap line in the dead of winter. Even after seven years of living in the remote Surprise Harbor, I was not prepared for the lonely life in a big city.

Soon after I arrived in San Francisco, I secured a job as an engineer in the powerhouse of the Southern Pacific Hospital on Fell Street. I found a place to live a short distance away in a cheap rooming house, and began my self-imposed sentence.

There was no shortage of pretty girls at the hospital where I worked, but I had pledged every spare dollar to Duke to help make the payments on the place we'd bought in Warm Springs Bay, so I did not feel free to pursue any of these girls and wine and dine them as they were accustomed. And too, if I should be taken with one of them, what would her reaction be to my life out in the Alaskan wilds? Being realistic, I knew that there was one in a thousand that would like the kind of life that I could offer.

But few men are immune to the effect a certain woman has upon them. I suppose that once in ever so many light-years a man chances across a woman that just suits him, one that has a touch of all the desirable little things he seeks out in the opposite sex, yet hardly ever expects to find. I was impatiently marking off the last days before I headed back to Alaska, when I met that special one for me. Her name was Barbara Martin and she was a nurse on the cardiac floor of the hospital where I worked.

The night before I was due to fly north, we had dinner at Barbara's apartment. When we had finished and moved into the front room with our coffee, Barbara looked at me, and asked, "When will you be through fishing this fall?"

"The twentieth of September. I'll fly back down here—"

She stood up abruptly and moved to the window to stare down into the street. "I don't want to wait until September," she said suddenly. "I think I'll just go back to Alaska with you now."

I didn't say anything for a long minute; I sat there trying to decipher the remark. "Is this an illicit relation you're proposing," I asked at last, "or honorable marriage?"

"Honorable marriage," she said, looking straight at me.

"You're serious?"

"Serious."

"Why, this is so sudden," I said, "I hardly *know* you!"

"Be serious!" she said.

"Look, Barb," I said, "I told you a little about the financial shape I'm in last night, but I didn't tell you the half of it. It's out of the question. Why, I've just got enough money to get back to Alaska and fill the fuel tanks on my boat. If I hit a big season this summer I might get out of debt . . . maybe this fall. . . ."

"Maybe you just don't want to be tied down," she said.

"No, it isn't that at all. But I just don't see how—"

"It's simple," she said. "I've got to give them two weeks' notice at the hospital; you can keep working until the first of May. We'll quit, get married by a judge— that won't cost much—then head for Alaska. Simple, huh? We'll go fishing on your boat and make a pot of money this summer, then we'll stay up there in your Warm Springs Bay, and build a nice big house. We'll hunt and trap in the winter—and raise a mess of big club-footed boys. How's that sound, Mister Wayne Short?"

She had made it simple, all right. But I wanted her to know a little of what she was getting into. "You know, we have terrible weather up there," I said. "In the fall it rains for days at a time, then it turns to snow, and it snows the rest of the winter. I live on Baranof Island, which is a hundred-mile string of nothing but mountains, and sometimes the snow gets fifteen feet deep. We spend most of the winter cutting firewood to keep from freezing to death, and the rest of the time shoveling snow to the outhouse in the brush. And, boy, is it cold sitting out there with a fifty-mile wind blowing down off the glaciers!

"You'd have to learn to cut wood, wash by hand, shoot brown bears that wander into the yard. You'll be eating venison, mountain goats, ptarmigan, ducks and geese, and fish in place of beef and pork. And if you fish with me on the boat in the summers, there's—"

"Sounds exciting," Barbara said. She rose and went to the phone and dialed long distance. After a few minutes, she said: "Mom? I'm getting married. Yes . . . the first of May, or thereabouts. Here in San Francisco, then we're going to Alaska to live. He's a commercial fisherman. No, I know I haven't written you about him, but I've known him for quite a while." She turned and rolled her eyes at me. "No, we won't have time to come back to Iowa, Mom, we have to get the boat ready to go fishing, you know. Well, I never did care for a big wedding. Yes, he's right here. Wayne, would you talk to my mother and reassure her that I'm not being kidnapped. . . ."

We were married two weeks later, and it certainly *wasn't* a big affair. It took place in the office of a traffic judge. When it was over, we booked passage to Seattle on a milk train that took twenty-some hours. But we didn't care.

We stayed overnight in Seattle, then flew to Juneau the next morning aboard a Pan American plane. The following day we flew the hundred-odd miles out to Warm Springs Bay in an Alaska Coastal Service Grumman Goose. As we came across Admiralty Island, Baranof Island loomed ahead of us, its ragged, snow-capped spires jutting high in the blue sky. "Look, Barb," I said, "see that deep cut over there in the mountains? That's home!" We crossed Chatham Strait, and the pilot laid the Goose on its side and slid down into the mouth of Warm Springs Bay.

I had planned on surprising the folks, but Barb would have none of that, and had insisted that I write and prepare them for her appearance. Ma and Pap were waiting on the airplane float to catch the plane. The pilot taxied up, cut the throttle, and we drifted in toward the float. Pap caught the wing pontoon, pulled us in, and made the lines fast. When we were out, I introduced Barb to the folks, then helped the pilot unload our luggage.

As we walked up the float toward the dock ramp, I asked Ma, "Where's Duke and Dutch?"

She looked embarrassed, and said, "Oh, they're acting silly!" As we came onto the boardwalk the boys peeked out from behind one of the buildings, giggling and pointing at Barb. Duke had a long beard, and wore a sheepskin coat turned inside out. On his head was a fur cap, and he wore a set of those wax teeth that stuck down over his lower lip. And as Barb studied this pair in astonishment, Duke poked his head out a little farther, crossed his eyes, and said, "Is this'n yore new bride from th' States, Brother Wayne? She shore is

purty. I wonder if'n she'd like to kiss her new brother-
'n'law?"

Barb stood still, a glazed expression on her face. The
rest of us couldn't stand it any longer and broke into
laughter. Even Ma was grinning. "Pay no attention to
them, Barbara," she said. "They've been practicing in
front of a mirror for a week. Come on in the house."

But Duke wasn't about to give up a good thing, and
he and Dutch galloped around on the walk and every
now and then would peek through the windows at
Barb. Finally, Ma got her trusty broom and put an end
to it.

Barb and I moved our things into one of the cabins
and got settled. When she went into the bathroom and
saw the toilet and big wooden bath tub filled with hot
mineral water, I saw the surprised look on her face,
and thought that she must have been prepared to shovel
her way through the snow to the outhouse.

Ma had a big dinner that night, and the whole population of the village of Baranof came—nine people, including the Shorts. I was given all the local news:
hunting stories, trapping yarns, what boats had gone
down during the winter, and I entertained everyone
with my adventures in the States during the winter.
Afterward, Duke brought out several bottles of liquor
and we all went up the boardwalk to our tiny cabin to
hoist a few and to talk until three o'clock.

At five-thirty, Barb and I awoke to loud explosions on

the walk outside the cabin. "What on earth is that!" Barb asked, sitting bolt-upright in bed.

"Just Duke shooting the shotgun to wake us up for breakfast," I said, and got up.

"Does he do that *every* morning?" Barb asked.

I went into the bathroom and got into the tub of hot mineral water. I soaked luxuriously for twenty minutes, then dried off and dressed. Barb had gone back to sleep. I lifted the covers and smacked her across the fanny with the flat of my hand. "Daylight in the swamp, *cheechako!*" I yelled. "Hit the deck; the honeymoon is over and we have a boat to get ready to fish." She rolled over, groaned, and rubbed her eyes.

I left her getting up, and stepped outside to the boardwalk. Already the sun was trying to muscle its way over the mountains in the east. The crisp sea air still had the breath of winter in it and, after seven months in the city, it tasted mighty good. I propped a foot on the railing and lit a cigar. In this early morning stillness a multitude of sounds came; the chirp of an otter over near the falls; presently I heard the hysterical laugh of a loon, then out near the mouth of the bay a whale blew as it fed on herring, and the sun touched its spout of vapor. A bald eagle shrieked from the top of a tall spruce nearby, then all was quiet for a moment. It was good to be home again.

I stood there savoring the goodness of this moment, trying to hold it as one holds the first pangs of love.

My chest hurt from the happiness within me. I thought of my luck in finding a woman like Barbara. Last night, Duke had said to her: "When the new wears off and the boredom sets in, you'll leave. I'll give you a year at the most." Barb had answered: "I'll be here a year from now, smarty . . . and twenty years from now! How'd you like to make a little bet?" And deep within me I knew that she would be, too. She had been the one I searched for, for so long.

I was still standing there smoking and daydreaming when the door opened and Barbara stepped outside. She saw me and smiled, then came toward me, slim and straight in the early morning light. "What are you doing?" she asked. "Just thinking," I answered, taking her hand, and we began walking down the boardwalk toward Ma's for breakfast.

About the Author

WAYNE SHORT was born thirty-seven years ago on the Arizona Desert. "My dad was a wandering man," he says, "and during the depression years we just about wore out the western states. I can't remember all the different schools that I attended. During World War II, I served for the most part in the South Pacific, where I was attached to the amphibious forces, and made the island invasions of Iwo Jima and Okinawa."

Mr. Short comes from a long line of pioneering people. In 1856 his great-grandfather crowded his large family into ox-drawn wagons and headed west. They finally settled on the Red River in Texas, where they raised cattle and fought Comanches and Kiowas. Most of this indomitable little man's sons grew to be cattlemen, but one, Luke Short, sought out the boom towns of the West, and was to become one of the most well-known gamblers and gun-fighters of that era.

The next two generations of Shorts turned west and north, seeking new country—"so I guess it was natural that my family would end up in The Last Frontier."

Mr. Short has worked as a trapper, bounty hunter, cannery tender skipper, and commercial fisherman. At present he owns and operates a fishing vessel named the *Seal*. About nine years ago he began to write and has sold short stories and outdoor articles.

Today he and his wife live in Warm Springs Bay, on Baranof Island, where the population is now sixteen—all Shorts. They have three sons, Mark, Mike, and Luke, who is named for his illustrious ancestor of frontier fame. Mr. Short's wife teaches the older boys with the aid of the Calvert Home Study Courses and they usually get to town about once a year.